THE LOGOS OF THE SOUL

DUNQUIN SERIES 2

THE LOGOS OF THE SOUL

by

EVANGELOS CHRISTOU

Spring Publications, Inc.
Dallas, Texas

The first Spring Publications edition in 1977 was photo-offprinted from
typography of the 1963 Dunquin Press edition set in Vienna.
Reissued 1987

Published by Spring Publications, Inc.; P.O. Box 222069; Dallas, TX 75222
Printed in the United States of America

Cover design and production by Maribeth Lipscomb and Patricia Mora

International Distributors:
Spring; Postfach; 8800 Thalwil; Switzerland.
· Japan Spring Sha, Inc.; 1-2-4, Nishisakaidani-Cho;
Ohharano, Nishikyo-Ku; Kyoto, 610-11, Japan.
Element Books Ltd; Longmead Shaftesbury;
Dorset SP7 8PL; England.

Library of Congress Cataloging-in-Publication Data

Christou, Evangelos, 1922 or 3-1956.
The logos of the soul.

(Dunquin series ; 2)
Reprint. Originally published: Zurich, Switzerland,
1976.
1. Psychology—Philosophy. I. Title.
BF38.C49 1987   150'.1   87-9645
ISBN 0-88214-202-X

EDITOR'S INTRODUCTION

THIS MONOGRAPH IS AN ESSAY in clarification. It attempts to think through a fundamental logic for psychotherapy and to separate this logic from that of the natural sciences and from that of philosophy. Psychotherapy has its own legitimate area of activity and its rights are based on the soul which, like the realms of matter and of mind, requires a logic of procedure, a book of words. The failure of psychotherapy to make clear its legitimacy has resulted in psychologies which are bastard sciences and degenerate philosophies. Psychotherapy has attempted to support its pedigree by appropriating logics unsuited for investigating its area. As these borrowed methods fail one by one, psychotherapy seems more and more dubious — neither good physics, good philosophy, nor good religion. Psychotherapists suffer from not being able to communicate about their area of reality in a scientific manner.

Psychologists evade this problem of fundamentals in accordance with their personal leanings. Those in the laboratory pattern themselves upon their colleagues whose operational systems come from the natural sciences; those following their medical associates do not seek beyond the heuristic and therapeutic. Others regret that psychology was ever split off from philosophy; they would reformulate the problems of the soul by means of strict linguistic analysis. The academies, wherever they have not succumbed to scientism in one form or another, simply describe and classify types, states, processes and functions. Last, least, and worst are those who are pleased to let things be. Contemporary Romantics, they prefer to keep psychotherapy occult, protecting the soul from the insult of intellectual clarification.

The problem which the author attacks in this monograph is the most difficult in psychology, more difficult even than the classical one of consciousness. It is so difficult because it takes up first principles, the very method by means of which any psychological investigation can be carried on at all. In this sense it is meta-psychology, but — and here is the new departure — it is not a metaphysical metapsychology which takes its premises from outside psychology.

As Freud, and Bleuler, too, looked beyond the psyche to ground their psychologies in the metaphysics of the last century's natural sciences, so today existential analysis looks beyond its own field to find ground in the metaphysical ontology of Heidegger. A pedigree for psychotherapy at any price! Of all the psychologies available to us now, only Jung's offers a metapsychology which is based not on statistics of probabilities, syllogisms, bio-chemical analysis, speculative metaphysics, but based upon and contained within psychology itself. The author follows Jung in taking *psychotherapy as the starting point for psychology*, and by developing his logos of the soul from the phenomenology of the soul itself. Like Jung, he always keeps in mind that for psychologists the psyche is the first reality. He writes: "The psyche is not inside man; it is we who are inside the psyche . . ."

Not only then does this essay drive straight to the heart of the psychotherapist's malaise, but it shows why this malaise, this sense of inferiority and illegitimacy, can never be cured by borrowing. Psychology does not become more scientific by becoming more like logic or like physics, says our author; it will become more scientific when it works out its own first premises and sticks to the categories of its own sort of reality. From within this reality, the reality of the psychologist as psychotherapist, the main problems of any scientific method are taken up. What is "meaning" in psychology? And how does it happen? What do we mean by "psychological reality", "psychological experience"? What is "observation" in psychology; is it introspection, or observation of behavioural acts, or neither? And how do we verify statements in psychology? What are the criteria for establishing an hypothesis without having recourse to the kinds of verification used in logic or in physics?

Throughout all this prodigious exercise of intellect, the author yet remains the practising psychotherapist, burning with the problems of the living soul. His use of reason is always for the sake of the psyche: ". . . although the clarification of such beliefs requires a great deal of clear thinking, it is not for the sake of the thinking but for the ulterior effect that the ideas arrived at will have on the soul. Put it slightly differently and say that part of the process of psychic development consists in making ideas that are hazy, unclear or outright unconscious, clear and concise."

He is thus a true heir of Socrates, of the theological philosophers of the North African shore, of the logical philosophers of Cambridge, and of Jung. The clarification of ignorance through reason must be for the sake of virtue, for the sake of the realisation of personality. Experience and revelation are the fathers of intellectual formulation, and the end result of intellect used rightly is therapy.

These were, in fact, the schools whose spirit he carries. Our author was Greek by birth and nature; he was raised in Alexandria, educated (by Wittgenstein among others) at Cambridge, and trained at the C. G. Jung Institute in Zurich.

Evangelos Christou is dead. He was killed on June 30, 1956, while a passenger in an open sports car in the Western Desert on the way back to Alexandria from Marsah Matrouh. There, he had spent a week working on this book. Part of it was found scattered at the scene of the accident. The authorities turned the papers over to the author's brother, Mr. Jani Christou. He worked on them in Alexandria and in Chios for many months, collating sentence by sentence the various manuscripts, stacks of notes, typescripts and jottings, until a final verbatim transcript of the first part of the planned work was ready for minor editorial revision by Mr. A. K. Donoghue and myself. Without Mr. Jani Christou's dedication to his brother's work it all would have been lost. The impulse to collect, to collate, and eventually to publish this work came originally from Mr. Kjell Nordenskjöld, Mme. Marie-Denise Tuby, and Dr. C. A. Meier .

The plan for the book shows that there was to be a final section, part of which was to amplify with case material what is here printed. Although some notes for this final section do exist, it was decided to produce the work as it stands and as Evangelos Christou left it. The editors have only made occasional corrections in language and tracked down some references. Thus the monograph, like his life, is a just-so story, a fragment to which the imperfections of a work-in-progress belong. But like a noble fragment of the antiquity from which he drew his source it is its own witness. Nothing else is needed for us to glimpse the value that is there.

It is not the first time that a brilliant young man — he was not yet thirty-four — leaves behind a seed, a logos spermatikos, that has its issue not in its creator's lifetime, but — as he states it himself in the last portentous phrase of the manuscript found where he died — "as it emerges from the soul of the knower and addresses itself to him and through him to others."

Early death of the gifted is an archetypal theme, iterating in the lives of gods, heroes, and geniuses. In itself early death does not establish genius; but when concurrent with any act uniquely creative we have indications of its mark.

We can conceive his death and this work in relation. Let us say the task killed him as similar tasks have taken the lives of other explorers and experimenters. *Let us say that there are perils of the soul for him who investigates its unknown reaches.* Alchemists, yogin, mystics, shamans record awareness of the mortal risks involved. When one reflects on the destinies of the pioneers of the psychonalytic movement, it would seem the same forces were at work. This is a basis of all esotericism; for even in the natural sciences the uninitiate must be kept from meddling with forces too potent for the public, the handling of which requires years of disciplined apprenticeship. Could we not conceive that the impact of his experience of the soul, channeled as it was for him through intellect rather than through visions or the body, implied his death? His death, a death from thinking to the limits of psychic reality, might be evidence indeed for the reality of the psyche, that theme which he made his life.

Evangelos Christou was aware of these perils and of the inner pressure on him. His insights raced against time. In a letter a few months before his death he speaks of "the problems of our destiny ... of extra-mundane life ... so sweeping and pressing, they claim so much of the whole man ..." He writes of an "ordeal", of passing "through the fire". He was intensely occupied with the realisation of personality, using the religious terms "salvation" and "redemption". All in all, considering his life and his work one is driven to conclude that something extra-mundane was at work which emerged in him, the knower, "and addresses itself to him and through him to others."

We are confronted with a *document humain* attesting to the mystery of the soul.

James Hillman

THE LOGOS OF THE SOUL

CONTENTS

PART I

GENERAL CLARIFICATION OF PHILOSOPHICO-SCIENTIFIC CONCEPTS

CHAPTER I

CHAPTER II

PART II

TOWARD A SCIENCE OF THE SOUL

CHAPTER III

CONTENTS

ADDENDA

INTRODUCTION

MUCH OF THE SIGNIFICANCE of a scientific psychotherapy will depend on the values we attribute to the things of the soul. But the concept of the soul, like that of spirit or of matter, has indefinite possibilities of interpretation and evaluation. These differences of meaning, moreover, may be due as much to divergences of theory *within* any given discipline, as to the differences which, in principle, distinguish from one another the various fundamental approaches to reality. For instance, what a certain philosopher or scientist will have to say about matter, soul or spirit will be governed, in the first place, by the logic of science or philosophy, as the case may be, and, in the second place, by the divergences which may arise between one philosophical point of view and another, one scientific theory and another.

Now the logic of science differs from the logic governing other fundamental conceptions of reality in that its truth values — however absolute the laws on which they are based may appear to be — are always open to the correction of experience. The principles governing any science of the soul, therefore, will be less concerned with definitions regarding the nature of the soul than with establishing experiential criteria by means of which any such definitions can be verified. Furthermore, these criteria and the fields they delimit will in turn depend on the conceptual system or method adopted to observe and formulate what is to be considered as psychological experience in the first place.

The meaning of a scientific psychotherapy, therefore, will depend on what it is able to discover of the mystery of psychic reality and psychological experience. But this mystery, like the other great mysteries of science, is an empirical unknown — possible of exploration and corrigible by experience.

Yet the criteria for scientific verification on the basis of experience depend not only on the observation of specific facts but, as we have seen, on the conceptual system which makes such observation possible at all. And what the principles of the method do not allow for cannot be discovered, confirmed or disproved by the science in question, no matter how exhaustive its observations. Thus, the rejection of a hypothesis on the grounds that it is not confirmed by the "facts" is of relative value; it must also be asked whether an appropriate method has been formulated establishing the nature of factual criteria for the case in question.

Hence the difficulty of developing and confirming scientific concepts is not only empirical, *i.e.,* owing to the indefiniteness and complexities of phenomenal reality, it is also logical, *i.e.,* owing to the need for adequate concepts with which to delimit this reality. And it is because the discovery of such concepts is so much more difficult that Russell made it the criterion of the highest scientific genius.[1] For it is far simpler to establish empirical propositions by using the old methods than to venture into the unknown by modifying the proved scientific methods of the day. The development of a logic of a new conceptual approach to reality usually meets, therefore, the opposition of science itself, as well as any of those disciplines upon whose territory the new methods encroach. Psychology, and in particular, the science and practice of psychotherapy is an important instance of this point.

2

Inspired and governed by the need for experiential verification, empirical psychology delimited the indefinite field of psychic phenomena to what could be observed or introspected, where these terms were used to cover the contents of sense perceptions and thought processes on the one hand, and the workings of instinct, affect and volition on the other. Thus, experimentation on behaviour patterns supplemented by introspection of inner states under varying circumstances threw a great deal of light on the nature of intelligence, the structure of preception, the function of the emotions and the workings of instinct and volition. Today the work of European and American psychologists on mental processes, character behaviour and motivation, not to mention the projective and intelligence tests used so extensively, testify to the fruitfulness of this approach to psychological phenomena.

But with Freud's discovery of psychological processes not so easily observed or open to introspection, other methods of investigation were required to meet the logic of the new situation. As a consequence, the scientific concept of what constituted psychological reality had to be enlarged; science had to admit the paradoxical existence of the unconscious, that is to say, processes of thinking, feeling, sensing, willing, and instinct life not open to direct observations. Moreover, the new discoveries pointed the way towards the possibilities of understanding such irrational processes as dreaming, the weaving of fantasies and the creative formation of myths. To empirical psychology was added a new science: that of depth psychology, with its practical implications covered by the term "psychotherapy" or "psycho-analysis". Psychotherapy was a revolution in method; as such it did not impose itself on empirical psychology but rather challenged some of the principles which scientific method in general had up to then left unquestioned.

This challenge was carried still further when Jung was able to show that the extraordinary effectiveness of dreams, fantasies, and visions was an irreducible quality of psychic processes whose significance could not be analysed into purely rational explanations. The meaning released by such experiences has always been recognised as a quality of life, but that it should be integrated by science, one of whose fundamental presuppositions is the rationality of the universe, whether physical or psychical, was a paradox more challenging than even the empirical paradox of the existence of the unconscious feelings, perceptions, thoughts and goals. The concept of the soul had thus once more to be modified to cover what can be considered as a new dimension, namely, the existence of an effective and significant but extra-rational psyche.

Psychotherapy, therefore, while greatly indebted to empirical psychology and to medicine, can be said to have gone beyond the consulting room and laboratory, to the extent that, going beyond itself, it has shown the way and created the need for a proper logic of the soul and an adequate method of exploration. The revolution effected by Freud's discovery, through the method of free associations, of the regions of the soul that lie beyond consciousness, was continued when Jung added to Freud's method those of amplification and active imagination which revealed the existence of an autonomous and extra-rational but none the less effective and significant psyche. And the work of both these pioneers points towards the need for a re-evaluation of the concept of psychological reality in the context of the life and thought of our day.

3

It is inevitable that the development of the science of psychotherapy should bring to the fore problems that were once exclusively the concern of philosophy and religion. For, unlike empirical psychology, the "matter" of a science of the soul is simply how people feel, talk, think and behave in life, not with what means they do this. And the interpretation of life has always been a prerogative of philosophy and religion to determine as it has been that of art to express it. Therefore, even though psychotherapy has the sanction which belongs to the authority of medicine it is difficult to see how such authority can be as valid in matters of the soul as in the those concerning the body. Moreover, if the concept of cure is more or less definable medically in terms of bodily or psycho-somatic standards, it is not so easily definable psychologically in so far as an essential element of psychological standards must necessarily include religious and philosophical considerations. When, for instance, a man suffering from difficulties of adaptation to life of a non-organic order undergoes a psycho-therapeutic treatment that leads to a better adaptation or cure, it can always be questioned in principle, either by philosophy or religion, whether such a cure has not been achieved at the price of a vitiation of attitude with respect to the values of the soul.

It is not surprising therefore to note that medical investigators who fathered modern psychotherapy justified their extra-medical investigations in the name and authority of science in general rather than medicine in particular. Both Freud and Jung, for instance, brought out clearly and repeatedly the differences that separate medicine from psychotherapy; yet, at the same time, both insisted on the scientific character of psychological research and practice, trying to free it as much as possible from philosophy, religion or art.

· In general therefore psychotherapy may be described as a science of life. But in that case it can be asked how much of life will be left if this science ignores religious, philosophical and artistic values, and if it does not ignore them, then in terms of what language can it talk about them at all. Faced with this difficulty, science tends to become either a sort of Procrustes bed forcing psychic reality to its size, or too philosophico-religious to be called a science at all. This is roughly the position that modern psychotherapy has worked itself into. On the one hand, Freud's scientific dogmatism recognises only the right of science as a valid instrument for the investigation of reality whether this is physical, psychic or even spiritual. On the other hand, Jung's scientific sincerity shows him how much science needs to change and modify its principles to meet the exigencies of a new order of reality, qualified as much by spirit as it is by instincts. But if the psychotherapist respects religious and philosophical statements as qualifiers of psychic life, irreducible and untranslatable into any other language, then how can he talk about them at all scientifically? Is not this a contradiction in terms? Indeed, it looks as though such a psychologist will be taking away with one hand what he gives with the other.

These considerations are sufficient to show us how irreconcilable is the point of view of science and that of philosophy and religion when it comes to matters of the soul. On the one hand science can no longer say that philosophies of life, religious experiences, artistic productions, are none of its concern, in so far as psychological statements must necessarily include references to the way people think, act and adapt to life; yet by giving such statements a scientific formulation, science tends by the force of its logic to create a standpoint that opposes the others. On the other hand it is clear that philosophy, religion or art cannot provide either separately or together modern man with a nourishment adequate to his life as it is being lived at present. They are mirrors of his disorientation rather than the effective guides, interpreters and qualifiers of his life. And the fact remains that in his disorientation and suffering he often prefers to go to the psychotherapist rather than to the priest or the philosopher.

Faced with this state of affairs, religion and philosophy can but affirm their points of view and go their way, anxious to ensure their survival, while science can only once more affirm its rights without being able to give philosophical or religious validity to its authority.

It is clear therefore how much we need a genuine logic of the soul and how difficult it will to be establish such a logic. For we are dealing with differences of principle that are irreconcilable while the languages they have given birth to are the only ones which are at present at our disposal. Therefore an adequate solution can only come when we are able to formulate a language which will issue from a principle that absorbs the others into itself and contains possibilities of integration denied them.

In this connection also it is to be noted that, while science cannot be denied a right it has conquered for itself in its triumphant victory over the symbolico-mythological interpretations of reality, the spirit of science is independent of this or that specific scientific conceptual system. It is only too tempting to transfer the authority of science to uphold this or that scientific theory. In its disinterestedness and integrity towards the correctives of experience and in its humility towards the relative values of its conceptual systems by means of which such experience is rendered possible and intelligible, the spirit of science can be found in all fields of life; as much in religion, philosophy and art, as in the experimental observations of the meaning of science. The spirit of intolerance and dogmatism can just as easily contaminate the scientist's attitudes to reality as it can a religious system of beliefs or a philosophical doctrine.

In matters of the soul, then, a science of life will require us to deal with an unknown that calls for commitments of faith, perseverance, and rectitude, which are virtues that qualify the spirit of science as well as philosophical quests, religious experience and artistic creation.

4

If psychotherapy in the name of science arrogates to itself the right to investigate the soul without at the same time making clear its own presuppositions, not only will it be guilty of betraying its own principles, but it will have ignored one of the distinguishing factors in the life situations which it seeks to "observe". One of the foundations of scientific knowledge is experiment, and as Freud pointed out, "the analyst is unlike other scientific workers in this one respect, that he has to do without the help which experiment can bring to research".[2] This becomes almost insuperable when we realise with Jung that the act of observation itself is impossible of objectivity in the case of psychotherapy as it can be for instance in that of astronomy or botany. The psyche cannot be isolated from its action and interaction with the environment, and contact with the psychotherapist creates a new relationship based on two psychic systems working upon one another. It follows that we must allow for modifications in the situation that are far less controllable and predictable than any which the rules of scientific experimentation can accept. If the scientist, for instance, lacks faith in the psyche, this lack of faith may seriously modify the psychological development he is observing and which might have been entirely different had the scientist, all other conditions being equal, had that faith. In psychotherapy, therefore, the human element cannot be ignored, in so far as what we bring of ourselves into the situation we are observing is a determining element in the course of further developments. Under such conditions, the "objective" validity of the "matter" the scientist is observing comes in question to a far greater degree than when scientific method is applied to the investigation of physical and bio-physical phenomena.

Thus, while it can be said that the method of psychological investigations is more or less objective, in the sense that it can be learned and applied by different people, the proof is subjective, in this sense that confirmation of the predictions made on the basis of the method are to a great degree a matter of personal experience. The proof of psychotherapeutic cures takes the form of a "testimony", a "witness", rather than of logical conclusions or empirical observations of an objective event.

In this specific sense religious and philosophical values in scientific observation no longer refer to unconfirmable propositions that science can reject as it must in the case of investigation of the physical world. For we are dealing here with a scientific probability that such beliefs, thoughts, feelings, do in fact influence psychological experience and therefore must be taken into account as qualifiers of the matter under observation. And we can only observe these *phenomena to the degree that we ourselves participate in them.* In other words, we cannot get more out of our matter than what we put into it; we can never arrive at spirit if we do not put spirit in from the beginning. Thus, if our psychological science leads to statements denying the truths of philosophy or religion, it is merely in a roundabout way coming back to the reflection of what it put into its matter from the start. The soul reflects the scientist's own credo. It is most significant in this respect that in spite of its tremendous progress science has not been able to add one iota to man's knowledge of himself, and seems to leave him qualitatively just the same as ever before, if not worse.

Science has no empirical reason for denying the action of spirit in the world. On the contrary, empirical science is itself based on an act of faith that can be overthrown any moment. There is no reason to reject acts of faith which could lead us to an understanding of other categories of reality than those of the physical world, merely on the basis that what has worked for the one should work for the other. Our act of faith therefore that the spiritual principle qualifies psychological experience is true to the spirit of science as well as issuing from a religious conviction and a philosophical inspiration which we have no reason to reject except by presuppositions that are as unproved and uncertain as those they seek to overthrow.

5

So long as science continues to experiment and philosophy to speculate, independently of the soul, the mind-body dichotomy will continue to sicken the wholeness of personality and the unity of life and spirit and thereby the cultural basis of modern life. And though it cannot be denied that they are very much concerned with the fate of the soul, philosophy and religion, even science cannot abandon their past commitments. Science still seeks to investigate psychological realities with models moulded for its investigations of physical phenomena; philosophy is still caught in formal, logical conceptual processes unable to pass over into the "life lived"; while religion, caught in an historical dogmatism and an unattainable transcendentalism, is unable to evaluate the empiricism and plasticity of psychic life.

Thus the problem that poses itself for psychotherapy is not one of science versus philosophy or religion, as Freud insisted, nor again is it a problem of compromise or mutual interchange of ideas, as modern syncretists would have. Rather, we are faced with the task of coming to terms with the fact impressing itself on us with growing urgency, that *the soul has a logic of its own* and an experience of its own not to be seized by languages appropriate to physical phenomena on the one hand, and to mental processes on the other. Therefore, it is not as scientists or philosophers or priests alone that we can hope to establish an effective language for psychological realities, but rather by bringing to bear on the unknown that confronts us the spirit that has sustained and inspired all these creative conquests of man in his fight against ignorance.

The establishment of an effective logos of the soul is as much a challenge to the power of our minds as it is a test of the spirit of our hearts. This task presupposes a phase of transition during which many old values will have to be abandoned to make room for new ones; this means undoubtedly a period of disorientation and of suffering, a crisis of the man as well as of the mind. Philosophical work, a spirit convinced of the religious significance of its commitments, and the inspiration of the artist as well as the ethics of the scientist with his disinterested pursuit of knowledge verified and corrected by adequate experiential criteria, are required to give validity and reality to the things of the soul.

As Jung rightly foresaw, our age is an age in quest of its soul. The anxiety, the despair, the suffering, and the disorientation of the inner life have deeply scarred the twentieth century. But as the Book of Job has shown us even illness and despair have their cosmic role. And have we but courage to admit our spiritual bankruptcy and suffer it in us, we may well discover the effective and rehabilitating power of the spirit working through the soul. Before the impersonal and intimate power of the spirit, there is no shame in the confession of weakness and failure. Rather, there is more reason to blame that arrogance that seeks to rule the world and human destiny on the basis of its own proud spirit, often hidden behind the pharisaic mask of what it purports to be the law of God. This refusal to confront reality for what it is comes often from the trust in science to heal all ills and to bring about a human Utopia on this earth. Naturally this goal is not achieved when the methods employed ignore spirit and soul as irreducible realities of experience to be accepted at their own worth, and not to be analysed away or deified into transcendent entities beyond the reach of mortals. On the contrary, it is now clear that this attitude has led us to the possibilities of complete and horrific self-destruction. The way of God is a mystery. Let us not say therefore that, through illness touched by divine Grace, there does not lie the possibility of redemption of the individual and of society — the restoration of the plenitude of life and the apocatastasis of their spiritual rectitude. The sufferings and disorientation of the soul, often too easily dismissed with the name neurosis, are facts that stare us in the face and either we recognise their challenge and stand in the reality of our age or else spend the rest of our lives devising means to deceive ourselves. In the recognition of this fact is truth, the truth of the living moment, and therefore too the possibility of a healing, a therapeia, and a response from the soul which we can hardly imagine.

Modern psychotherapy, if it is willing to recognise these problems as essential to any understanding of the science of life, cannot but be greatly enriched to the benefit of that science and of all those for whom science is not only a knowledge of the world acquired through thought or perception, but a knowledge lived. *Indeed, psychotherapy may well prove to be the prodigal son of its age.*

6

In the following pages an attempt will be made to clarify the principles on which a logos of the soul can be validly constructed. The confusion of claims and the mutual incompatibilities between scientific psychotherapy, religion, philosophy, and art, which we have briefly reviewed, make such a task an exceedingly delicate one. Psychological experience covers the whole range of life, both the world of dreams, fantasies and visions, what we may call the inner world, and that outer one of everyday reality. It seems extraordinary that science has for so long ignored the fact that both the inner and outer world are sources of experience, and has rather tended to see in them only the objects of perception or those of ideation. The idea and the thing perceived seem to be the only possibilities of reality open to science, while the thing experienced can only be understood scientifically by being translated into the object of a perception or the content of a conception.

Yet there is every reason to suppose that the concept of psychological experience should correspond to our idea of the soul in much the same way as physical perception corresponds to that of matter or conception corresponds to that of mind. Indeed, just as matter covers the class of material things, and just as mind covers that of ideas, so does soul cover the class of psychological experiences. In fact, it cannot be emphasised too much in view of the latest development of psychology, that the reality of psychological experience is more basic than that of perception or conception. The difference between a thinking automat or a photographic plate and a human being remains that indefinable something we call soul; this would mean that a human being is able to *experience* what he thinks or feels, where the concept "experience" means more than just perceive or think the content in question. And it is precisely this indefinable more that makes psychological experience a reality of its own. It is clear therefore that no science of the soul can claim any validity if it is not firmly rooted in a logic of such reality.

But, as we have seen, science does not mean only the possibilities of observation of a certain field of reality; it also implies a method of interpretation. Having delimited the field we intend to study and the principles which distinguish it from other fundamental categories of experience, we have still to say what system or method of interpretation is best adapted to the investigation of that field. In this connection, however, we come up against certain difficulties that do not exist in other fields which science investigates.

In the first place, for instance, it is clear from what we have already said that certain psychological processes release meanings that cannot be seized by a rational analysis or formulation. Yet, if we attribute an extra-rational significance to them we will be putting aside just that systematic use of reason that has helped us so much in overthrowing the symbolic, mythological, and hence unscientific, constructions of reality.

In the second place, the concept of unconscious psychic processes places us before the dilemma of having to admit the reality of things we have by definition no means either of observing or conceiving. Moreover, if we accept the validity of such a hypothesis, we would again be admitting the existence of a world of mythological and magical experience, the systematic denial of which is one of the foundations on which modern consciousness has been erected.

In the third place, the close connection which obtains between psychological transformations (cure) and the methods of analysis and observation applied, implies that even the initial scientific methods employed cannot ignore philosophical, religious, or artistic values, in so far as these can actively modify psychological processes in a way they do not, for instance, a mathematical proof or a physical experiment.

Finally, adaptation to life by an individual is inadequate as a criterion of psychological integrity and maturity in so far as these imply, firstly, an inner response and, secondly, a freedom of personality that is not verifiable by observation alone. A man may be very well adapted to social and professional life and yet inwardly be in a state of latent conflict. Hence, since the criterion of any scientific truth is confirmation by public observation, and since such confirmation, in the case of psychotherapy, takes the form of a private testimony in addition to the public observation, it is clear that the concept of therapy will acquire an elasticity of meaning unknown to medicine. Moreover, since a proper logic of the soul implies also the universality of its first principles, it follows that these must offer effective interpretations of psychological experience as it applies to the adult and generally healthy man as well as to the sick and so called neurotic ones.

While Part I will take up the problem of an adequate delimitation of psychological realities and its principles, Part II of this work will contain a discussion of the method, and Part III will contain illustrations from case material of the results of this orientation of principle and method in the actual psychotherapeutic situation which remains the touchstone of all discussions and the anchor of all theory.

The results of this work will enable us to reformulate briefly in Part IV some of the perennial problems that confront the evaluation of the human personality crucified between spirit and instinct, mind and body, yet containing within itself the principle of its unification and the meaning of its life and its redemption. *Modern man thirsts for the scientific justification of what he feels dimly within him and which science at present cannot adequately formulate.* The scientific formulation of these psychological realities does not mean that any of the perennial problems of man are thereby solved. It means only that they are given a contemporaneous meaning. And it means that science itself becomes, whether it cares to admit it or not, an active factor in the problem of truth not only as an objective fact but as a redeeming and subjective transforming power, experienced by man who, as the old truth will have it, is made in the image of the Creator and contains in his heart the principle of a trans-human integrating and redeeming spirit, by which, in ultimate analysis, science itself with all its Promethean courage must be finally justified.

---

[1] Russell, B.: *Mysticism and Logic,* Pelican edn., p. 45
[2] (Quote untraced.)

PART I

GENERAL CLARIFICATION OF PHILOSOPHICO-SCIENTIFIC CONCEPTS

CHAPTER I

1: SCIENCE AND PHILOSOPHY

THE SEVENTEENTH CENTURY announced the separation of nature from religion and the possibility of observation of natural facts unencumbered by theological speculations. With the empirical confirmation of the Copernican system and its victory over the Ptolemaic, astronomy had already set a notable example in freeing science from the cosmological and symbolic interpretations to which it had been subject. Galileo in Italy and Bacon in England were chiefly responsible for the establishment of scientific method with its emphasis on observation and experimentation. But, at the same time they set up the method, they developed the philosophical principles which could permit a separation of the "divine" from the "natural" and thus justify the new outlook. Accordingly both the concept of nature and that of spirit were radically modified. Nature was subject to law; law was necessary and objective, connecting one event to another and could account for the various phenomena observed in the heavens and on earth. Thus, there was no need to resort to transcendental explanations to explain the mysteries of this cosmos, only to look for the law. And when the genius of Newton in England and that of Descartes in France discovered the possibilities of formulating natural law in terms of mathematical equations, it followed that the concept of natural law was further specified as tending towards simplicity and economy of means, as perfect in its order and as harmonious and inevitable in its consequences as mathematical thought itself. From the seventeenth century onwards, therefore, the concept of Nature implies an orderly, perfect, simple, and harmonious universe, sustained by invariable laws expressible in mathematical equations, and subject to observation, discovery and control by methods devised by man's reason — the light of Nature.

As a result, man acquired a freedom he never before possessed. Spirit came to mean more and more the spirit of human thought and human reason. The spirit of the divinity was not, of course, denied, but it was respectfully banished to abstract and incorporeal regions beyond the boundaries of the observable cosmos. And though the spirit could still be the pious object of a religious attitude or a philosophical system it was to be differentiated from the "empirical" and "natural" reality around us; and this differentation was effected and sustained by reason with its indefinite possibilities of mathematical conception and experimental observation. It was inevitable that this new attitude to reality should bring about a re-evaluation of the nature of truth.

In the first place, the age old problem of the deceptive and irreal senses aquired new meanings; for, the evidence of the senses became both the source of our new knowledge as well as the source of our incertitude concerning this knowledge. In the second place, the truths of the self-evident mathematico-philosophical axioms acquired the aura of the absolute and with his new ways man could depend with certainty on the truth revealed by the propositions and axioms of the exact sciences. Hence the new methods for the observation and investigation of nature were influenced by those disciplines where the concepts provided the greatest certainty at that time, namely, geometry and arithmetic.

However, the uncertainty concerning the evidence of the senses did not prevent man from using them to his utmost and constantly devising means to extend their range. Thus, while the reports of the senses were all and one uncertain, nevertheless the world they revealed was real enough, and it was this reality which preoccupied the new spirit. And paradoxically enough, while the notions of the mind were most certain, it was not at all clear what was the nature of the realities, if any, which they expressed. There was division of opinion with no way of finding out. However certain the most self-evident propositions were, they could not guarantee the real, while however uncertain were the reports of the senses they at last revealed to us something of some sort of reality within reach, *i.e.*, confirmable by experience common to all. Accordingly the problems of spirit and the ultimate nature and truth of the world of ideas became more and more problems of logic and less and less capable of influencing ways of life. And when it did come to spirit and life there was talk of mysticism, faith, intuition, which concepts had however no point in common with reason and the new empiricism.

Thus philosophy travelled one way and science another. Yet, today, the classical scientific concept of an objective field of sense-observable events taking place independently of the observer and conforming to laws waiting to be discovered has given way to a far more involved notion of the relations that obtain between the observer, the method or instrument used, and the thing observed. It is a debatable point whether the laws of science are discovered at all, or whether they are not put into nature by absolute, the necessary, the true. From discussions as to whether there are any natural laws that are both *a priori* and synthetic, that is to say, contain absolutely certain information about events in the world, we pass to statements as radical as those that assert that all empirical laws are mere statistical prohabilities. From the formal point of view, Wittgenstein was able to say, "The law of causality is not a law but the form of a law".[1] In *Space, Time and Gravitation*, Eddington confessed — "... we have found that where science has progressed the farthest, the mind has regained from nature that which the mind has put into nature",[2] and "It is one thing for the human mind to extract from the phenomena of nature the laws which it has itself put into them; it may be a far harder thing to extract laws over which it has no control. It is even possible that laws which have their origin in the mind may be irrational and we can never succeed in formulating them".[3] These considerations are the result the mind observing her. Furthermore, the classical concept of law has also suffered considerable modifications. It has lost its status of the of a long and gradual development of scientific exploration and should not be confused with similar statements made by speculative philosophy: to have introduced them therefore before they were called for by the facts would simply have paralysed scientific research.

Thus, though he has reached the frontiers of the explorable, the scientist's interest in first principles is still motivated by the possibilities they may offer for further empirical exploration. He is less naive about the one true method and more willing to look around for new points of view; but these must be rooted in a reality that can be verified and of which he can make confirmable predictions. The philosopher on his part is also facing the limits of his world. Reality has slipped through his systems; yet wisdom is still pursued by means of the analysis and manipulation of logic and language. Although philosopher and scientist are conscious of this dichotomy, each still seeks his own interest. The tree of knowledge that nourishes our modern world draws its waters from two streams flowing parallel and there is as yet no means of uniting them: the first — formal, logical, mathematical; the second — empirical, observational, statistical.

Before going more extensively into this situation it will be necessary to say something of the methods that underlie the bulk of scientific and philosophical knowledge since the Cartesian revolution. The analytic or synthetic methods as they have been called consist, in the former case in the analysis and reduction of complex phenomena to simpler denominators, and in the latter case in the construction from simple premisses of more complex wholes. These methods have been used as successfully in the analysis of empirical phenomena as in the elaboration and construction of mathematical and logical systems. Yet, if they have proved to have been and still to be principles of exploration of incalculable value in the exact as in the natural sciences, *they have also been the occasion for the entertainment of expectations that can never logically be fulfilled.* And, in so far as these expectations have a direct bearing on the presuppositions of science in general and the methods and principles of psychology in particular, it will be necessary to examine them more closely in connection with these methods.

2: THE ANALYTIC AND SYNTHETIC METHODS

In the great deductive systems the absolute, simple, or what today would be called the axiomatic, atomic propositions form the starting point of a chain of reasoning which links the various units to one another into smaller or larger wholes, which we may call complex. The simple proposition considered in the past as indivisible and self-evident is today indivisible in the sense that it cannot logically be defined in terms of any other proposition or group of propositions belonging to the system in question: its self-evidence is carried over to its form and no longer belongs to its so-called transcendental content to be grasped by intuition or any other special faculty. Thus, certainty of knowledge belongs to the form, while doubt is the prerogative of propositions about the empirical world and is measured statistically.

In the latter case, moreover, the simplicity of any proposition about the world is understood as referring to the content of a proposition that can be verified by a sense observation. When therefore modern science talks of facts, no matter how complex these may turn out to be, they are all and one reducible by definition to perceptual observations more or less difficult but possible. The difficulties encountered in the case of the indefinitely large and the indefinitely small remain with respect to the instruments employed, empirical. Whoever, therefore, uses the concept of empiricism in our times intends just such phenomena observable by the senses, or at any rate the possibility of their coming under observation either by means of better instruments or better means of displacement of the observer.

Now the connection which obtains between the complex and the simple propositions which constitute the elements of knowledge is, in the case of philosophy and metaphysics, a formal logical connection while in the natural sciences it is a causal principle of sequences based on statistical probabilities. Today it is clear that all scientific laws are ultimately matters of statistical probability. The simpler the formulation and the greater the number of facts a scientific hypothesis can correlate the higher the degree of its statistical truth. Modern science tends towards the formulation of the fundamental law which will be able to comprise the whole of the empirically known universe. Yet, even though modern science were to succeed, this law would never be more than a very high type of statistical probability. Thus, in spite of its immeasurable fruitfulness, it will nevertheless remain empirical, that is to say, in theory it will always be possible to overthrow it on the basis of some event occurring in the world which it cannot explain. Of course, the higher type generality of the law, the more difficult it will be to find a disconfirming instance. But difficult as this may be, it is not *impossible,* and the fact that the law *can* be overthrown is highly challenging.

A hope can be discerned in these problems which, though it has no foundation in fact and is not warranted by logic, nevertheless plays an exceedingly important role in sustaining the interest in these methods of acquiring knowledge adopted by the exact and the natural sciences. This expectation which always seems near fulfilment but is actually never fulfilled will be referred to as the *knowledge myth* and discussed in what follows.

3: THE KNOWLEDGE MYTH

Knowledge itself is no myth. The present circumstances of our lives, the effectiveness of scientific knowledge, the developments in logical, mathematical, and philosophical thought, do not permit of statements questioning its reality. When we talk of a *knowledge myth,* we refer to a hope which is closely connected to the methods of acquiring knowledge which these methods nevertheless do not seem able to fulfil. And moreover, strangely enough, repeated failure seems to have little effect on the tenacity with which this hope is held or the manner in which it tends to repeat itself. In fact it seems that it is of the essence of the myth that it should flourish on a constant shifting of meanings below the surface of clear and logical expositions. The detection of this shifting of meaning is a philosophical experience of its own which would take us beyond our subject. All we can do at present is to discuss those points which concern us in general and the specific form which they take in psychology.

As we have seen, science on the one hand, logic and metaphysics on the other, proceed by reducing the complex to the simple and vice versa. This method proves its value provided we remain within the respective fields under investigation. Thus, simpler empirical facts can be related to more complex *facts,* while simpler logical forms can be shown to underlie more complex *logical* relations, or vice versa. Now the problem of the nature of the connection that obtains between the empirical order of reality on the one hand and the logical order on the other is one of the important aspects of the general problem of the interrelation, if any, between body and mind. And in this connection it is interesting to note that philosophical schools tend to orient themselves according to whether they consider complex mental "facts" as ultimately translatable into simpler physical facts ("after all aren't mental facts really sorts of physical facts?"), or conversely whether the complexity and reality of the phenomenal universe is not "really" an aspect of the original unity and simplicity of ideas, that is, of Mind. Yet the simple physical fact in spite of all efforts finally fails to explain the elusive mental "fact", while the quest continues for the logical proposition that is not only self-evident but tells us something about the world. Like a fishing net whose spacings are too large, the conceptual systems in vain try to catch the contents of physical reality.

In spite of this dichotomy, the hope remains throughout the various philosophical schools of thought that one day the problem will be solved one way or another, that is to say, that we will either discover the connecting principle, or else know why and how there can be no such principle.

The body-mind dichotomy, therefore, is connected to the basic problems of philosophy and metaphysics concerning the nature of ultimate reality in this way: there is always the possibility that through logical analysis or factual investigation we will be able to discover something of the truth at the origin of this world. And this preoccupation in spite of epistemological considerations to the contrary distorts the logic of both science and philosophy in terms of a hope that with every successful conquest whether of the world of mind or that of matter-of-fact, we will be nearer this ultimate reality be it called God, Being, Mind, Reality, Matter, Energy, or any other name we give it.

Consider for instance the following statements made by Francis Bacon three hundred and fifty years ago, as valid today as they were when he first wrote them: "So it is with contemplation; if a man begins with certainties, he shall end in doubts; but if he will be content to begin in doubts *he shall end in certainties.*"[4] With what such certainty is connected can be clearly seen when he says, "... but when a man passeth further" (*i.e.,* is not content to dwell on second causes) "... and seeth the dependence of causes and the works of providence; then, according to the allegory of the poets, he will easily believe that the highest link of nature's chain must needs be tied to the *foot of Jupiter's chair.*"[5]

One way or another, generation after generation of men have reiterated this hope and none seems to have been able to realize it. It looks as though indeed it is an allegory of the poets. Yet this failure has not prevented real work from being accomplished. On the contrary it seems as though much of the success of science depends on the mobilisation of energy attached to this hope in order to sustain the often hard and thankless task of painstaking scientific enquiry. This hope serves the purpose very much, as Plutarch tells, as religious symbols served in the task of subduing and cultivating the earth: they capture man's interest and direct and sustain his work. In this case, it is not the earth that man is cultivating, but the unknown in nature and in himself.

Thus, behind the advances of scientific and philosophical knowledge stands the mind-body dichotomy which is closely connected to problems of ultimate reality which in turn reveal to us the secret hope that man can somehow resolve the mystery of the world and of the spirit. Indeed it seems as though it is precisely this hope that has sustained much of man's work in the related fields of phenomenal realities. Yet it is quite appropriate to ask why after Kant's epistemological critique such expectations still persist. One of the answers to this question is today becoming clear in much the same way as the problem of observation and experimental interference with nature is also being clarified. The separation of spirit from nature which was indispensable for scientific knowledge left behind it a problem of justification that has still to be met. For whatever the drawbacks of the old traditional orders they did at least provide an adequate source of justification for human enterprise. By separating the human from the divine, man had also to assume the burden of justification for whatever enterprises he undertook. Moreover, his interference and experiments with nature are based on principles that do not carry within themselves any justification that is either self-evident or revelatory. On the contrary the fact that advance in knowledge has not led to better human beings but has left human nature as much at the mercy of its irrational passions as before, is disturbing evidence of the incompleteness of the ways chosen by the West to pursue wisdom. The need to get back to spirit therefore, after first having clearly separated it from nature, indicates that there is a human problem involved which can best be described as a problem of justification between man and spirit that weighs heavily on the former in spite of epistemological considerations and leaves him no peace either to enjoy his knowledge or to understand better the mysteries of his own existence. For it is clear that if man's ways do not contain their justification they can hardly be expected to be justified in terms of those very principles which they originally questioned.

Modern thought is acutely conscious of this problem; for, whether we regard spirit as simple thought or as a transcendental qualifying principle, the moment we start thinking and altering the course of events in the world by means of this thinking, then we have to face the problems of justification created by our activities in the worlds of animate and inanimate nature. Yet the only attitude which the scientific mind seems to have adopted before this challenge is to hope on an act of faith with respect to its methodologies that eventually those methods themselves will lead to the knowledge which will finally justify and thereby remove the burden of responsibility of the world and its destiny which it has so rashly taken upon itself to carry. It will therefore be necessary to look a little more closely at the problem of justification created by the application of experimental interferences to better understand the conditions to be fulfilled by a psychological methodology.

4: OBSERVATION AND JUSTIFICATION

Any attempt to observe a cross section of the flow of phenomena in the world, itself being another such flux, necessarily introduces a change into what is to be observed. In the world of ordinary physics such changes are not appreciable, but in micro-physics experimental intervention is seen as changing the field in question so that it never appears as it would have been had there been no intervention. Moreover, as such interventions are the only ways we can investigate phenomena, it follows that we never are observing an objective event but only an objective event in so far as it has been modified by our experimental interference and our subjective presuppositions. Thus we observe conditions that we have in a sense ourselves already helped to determine in a given way. It follows that the world is never seen as what it is but only as what it *becomes* once we decide to observe it and hence modify it by whatever means we employ and whatever interferences we create. If these conditions are true for micro-physics and in a lesser sense for physics, how true they must be in the sciences of biology and psychology. There "matter" is studied alive and is exquisitely receptive to any form of intervention. The problem created by this situation is of great importance. For, if the world is being constantly modified by the very fact that man is observing and thinking it, man assumes a responsibility for the course of events far beyond his actual capacity to shoulder. To maintain under such circumstances that man alone is observing the world is to make him into a very different being from what he thinks he is. In fact he assumes a cosmic responsibility equal to that of a creator god. And it implies moreover that, were man to break down under the burden, the whole world would also break down with him. But if man is not the only observer of the universe then it follows that some trans-personal spirit is not only observing this world but is also in it, that is to say, modifies it by the very fact of its being under observation. And if we answer that it may be observing the world without being in it or interfering in any way, then who is? For clearly the world is being modified and has been modified by interventions of a trans-personal order: it is not only the scientist who has changed the world but also and above all its prophets. And these, whatever the ultimate validity of their inspiration, were clearly working in an impersonal context. It is with difficulty that the scientist can avoid the conclusion that trans-personal forces are modifying the world and that God cannot be regarded any longer as a transcendental principle beyond this world or a sort of kindly all-forgiving father. He is in the world in a way that the philosophical theory of immanence had never dared to hope. The consciousness of the prophets, the consciousness of philosophers, is itself a force which while observing and commenting on the world transforms it, just as the scientist himself is transforming it with his controlled experimental interventions.

We should not, therefore, be surprised by the uncertainty, anguish, and god-almightiness of the spirit of our times: uncertainty and anguish because, since man depends on himself alone and since he knows how irrational and undomesticated are his instincts, he is not at all comforted by the power that he is acquiring through scientific knowledge, and for which he is alone responsible; god-almightiness because his vision of the cosmos and his power over it have enormously increased. With this he assumes a role he is not fitted to play alone. He therefore seeks to pass the burden of the responsibility on to someone who can. Who else can that be but the Creator Himself? And so part of the spiritual conflict in which the modern man is caught consists in finding ways and means for shouldering the responsibility for this situation on to God. For, if God is responsible for this state of affairs He can also redeem it. This is a very old idea which, however, involves a confrontation with God on a very different basis from that which classical science approached Him. Man cannot make God responsible for the cosmos and still go on digging it up and creating havoc everywhere. If, on the other hand, man refuses to recognise God's responsibility with his own, he stands alone and under the unenviable danger of disintegrating from the strain of having to carry the world. These are not theoretical speculations but the immediate consequences of the scientist's very real position with respect to human destiny and its problems, and which the atomic age has served to confirm. It is important to notice in this connection the counter tendency to make the devil responsible for the evil in the world. But the problem remains the same. If the devil is made responsible for this state of affairs this does not in the least relieve man of the burden of having to face his share of the work. This sort of move tends to push the issues but one step further. If man is not entirely responsible and if this responsibility falls in part to God and in part to the devil then on whose side is man? For it is clear that by the fact that man can modify the world and the course of events his choice of sides will have a corresponding influence on the issues which are being worked out.

It is now clear what lies behind problems of justification, namely, the very real responsibility that falls with all its fatal weight on both philosopher and scientist. This responsibility is not just an ethical concern outside their specific interests and activities; it is woven into the fabric of science and philosophy. It effectively qualifies and thereby modifies the world and its observers by the very method of observation which by its systematic and widespread interferences is itself another process that cannot but change those it seeks to know.

As psychology implies a method with processes of observation and interference, and as it also deals with the most responsive of all matters, the soul, it must necessarily take into account, from the outset, the philosophical and ethical factors involved in the application of the method and without which it risks vitiating its results. This in turn would risk vitiating the contents of its theories with respect to the realities it seeks to discover, by the very process with which it proposes to carry out these investigations.

5: THE SOUL AS MYSTERY

The advance of science by the confirmation of its methods with tangible discoveries created the hope that the world could be changed for the better and explained on the bases of what was discoverable and knowable. On the basis of the knowledge derived form the natural sciences we could harness the forces of nature and build a more comfortable world to live in; on the basis of knowledge attained through the exercise of reason we could disclose the hidden springs of moral actions, the sources of will, the spirit behind genius and personality. By this means science hopes to be in a position to create an ethically superior culture, an intellectually enlightened one, an artistically creative one and a materially comfortable one. Within the framework of the hopes raised in his ideology, the scientist does not aspire to the knowledge of ultimates, but he does hope that, if he can establish the laws that obtain between things, both of the same and of different orders, then, within the limits of his humanity, he may consider himself as contributing positively towards the problems of existence.

Today we are beginning to realise that the situation is not so simple. The world is shaped and distorted as much by what is ignored as by what is known, by what is unknowable as by what is knowable. The unknowable somehow exerts an appreciable influence in the world. And our attitudes and philosophies with respect to this unknowable have a great deal to do with the orientation and development of knowledge, and of the world as we make it. According to whether we believe a thing to be knowable or not, so will our efforts be modified. Moreover, a possible neglect or misunderstanding concerning the unknowable does not thereby mean that it will not continue to act as a potent force in the formation and transformation of the world, in forms or effects which are knowable and empirically within our reach. We are not so certain now that, in spite of the epistemological delimitation of the boundaries of the knowable and the unknowable, the latter will remain quiescent in the transcendent heavens or for that matter in the depths of the earth, where it must by force take refuge.

Our attitude to the unknowable is a fact in life we cannot analyse away into problems of philosophy, or relegate to the concern of religion divorced from the banalities of everyday life. These same banalities accumulate to form an underlying attitude or philosophy of life. When this attitude is derived from a spirit built on the rejection of the unknowable as a fact in the world, when moreover a part of this unknowable is also God or ultimate reality, so too, the actions, thoughts, loves, emotions, passions, hopes and fears of that life will be determined in their contents and their forms accordingly.

It is not surprising, therefore, that with the inauguration of the new era in the early XVIIth century, mystery, which in the past had revolved around this recognition of the unknowable as a fact in life and sought to come to terms with it, fell into disrespect. It is not that the unknowable was rejected, but that the *logical* distinction which was made served to remove from men's sight the fact that, though the unknowable could not be known, it nevertheless could be *experienced* and had an effect on people which could not be ignored. As a result of this partiality for reason at the expense of the experience of spirit, mystery became unreal, fantastic: a world of poetic license, of superstition, of fantasy, to be explained or else to be dismissed by reference to the new methods of reason and the evidence of the senses. This is not to say that the reality of inner experiences was denied, or for that matter the existence of superior spiritual forces, but these, to be intelligible and acceptable, were referred to the logic of intellect or the laws of nature, as man conceived them in accordance with the principles of his methods. Mystery as an experience, which was of the soul and of the spirit, was secularized and rationalized. It became the logically unknowable, the transcendental beyond experience and formulation; or else, the empirically unknowable, that which was mysterious only because we were ignorant of the causes which remained however within our possibilities to discover and was the legitimate object of our investigation.

But no sooner had the age whose philosophy of life rested on the "notions of the mind and the reports of the senses" set in than the age of the exotic also announced itself.

Fascinated by mysteriousness, the age of reason could not resist an insatiable curiosity for the remote, whether in time or in space. From the fantastic stories of eastern wisdom, whose literature had begun to be translated, to baroque mystery novels the world of the unknown fell like an incense cloud on the culture that was to see the liberation of man from superstition and from the tyranny of nature's inimical forces. In the heart of the new culture a battle between the light and the dark was engaged, two sides that belonged equally to it. Yet, it was not so much that the light was good and the darkness evil in an ethical or religious sense, though sides were taken and held with all the passion which belongs to religious issues. Light, the light of nature, was the light of knowledge and progress, of that enlightenment that comes to us through the exercise of reason and observation; darkness was that twilight world of mystery and poetic imagination, that night of gross superstition and incense-burdened religions that becloud the mind and numb the heart.

In psychology a long line of illustrious names marks the various phases of this battle. From the side of science, from Mesmer's first empirical beginnings in animal magnetism — "that NATURE AFFORDS A UNIVERSAL MEANS OF HEALING AND PRESERVING MEN." [6] — through Braid's "nervous sleep" with its psychological aetiology, Bernheim's theory of suggestion introducing psychological causation, Janet's theory of dissociations, and finally Freud's theory of repression and discovery of the unconscious, the story shows a common thread: the attempt to apply the methodology of sciences as it had developed and proved itself in the natural and exact sciences to the *phenomena* of the soul. Thus, even when science had to accept a purely psychological aetiology, nevertheless the *logic in which its premises were formulated belonged to the logic of reason and sense observation.*

From the side of medical philosophy Stahl, Carus, Groos, Ideler, and Hartmann were a few among those who intuited the psychic factors involved which science could not as yet formulate within its methodology. But the possibility of coming to grips with the world of mystery and the unknowable as a scientifically valid fact came into sight only at the turn of the twentieth century when it was formulated empirically under the name "the unconscious".

But even this concept was by no means satisfactory. The methods of science did not do justice to the facts as the philosophers saw them. They felt and still feel that science has not sufficiently taken into account the extent to which it has itself to change in order to adapt itself to the nature of the facts it now seeks to cover. Following Bergson's criticism of science and his concept of the "elan vital", an important group of people believe that science will never be able to integrate that element of the living quality in nature and in the soul, as long as it remains what it is and is unable to formulate a method appropriate to such matters. It is not without irony that the severest critics of the psychologies of the unconscious are today the philosophers, those, that is, who did most toward its recognition; while the scientists who approach the concept as a purely empirical, heuristic principle for investigating human behaviour end up with all sorts of philosophical speculations. Yet, the philosophers today are still caught in the meshes of their own thought forms, and though they may well intuit and conceptualise the unconscious as an important subject for philosophical discussion, they are still unable to pass from the concept to the fact without doing an injustice to the logic of the conceptual approach itself. And so, their work, however brilliant and important in its field, remains theoretical and does not touch the modern man as he feels it should. It fails to satisfy the needs of the living soul.

Today, the world of mystery, the dream, the fantastic, have all undergone a considerable if not frightening metamorphosis. No longer contained within the innocuous mystery literature of this age, it has now been sanctified by psychology and confirmed by science. Yet, by a strange irony of fate, science itself has become the mystery of mysteries. Not only does it demand years of specialised study, but surrounded by myriad precautions and under the jealous guardianship of the state, it is doubly inaccessible to the layman, and carries his most fantastic imaginings, hopes, and fears. Nor is it very far from the truth to say that his wildest dreams have every chance of being confirmed in reality. Thus, what the psychologists have called the unconscious has entered life, is all about us, a grim reality handling weapons of unimaginable power: mystery is a fact and this fact overshadows life as never before.

It is clear therefore that, although the concept of the unconscious, intuited by the philosophers, defined and described by the psychologist, has not solved the problem posited by the existence of the unknowable, the unknown, the mystery, it has put a lot of water in our wine. It points to a factor which man has tended to overlook: a considerable source of mystery is man's soul itself. The soul has not yielded to scientific method as nature has done, nor as the mysteries of ideas and numbers had revealed themselves to the reasoning mind. Though the soul can be in part thought of, in part measured, as a phenomena of life processes, this is not by far the whole story. Nor can religious sentiment and noble aspiration, of which both scientist and philosopher have given ample evidence, suffice to justify their methods and the hopes based on them. The soul remains the great unknowable.

In this connection the various spiritualistic philosophies, psychic research movements, and esoteric societies, with which our culture teems, are instructive evidence of the need to recognise psychic reality. And while they often make an honest attempt to deal with the soul, nevertheless the language at their disposal remains largely conditioned by all the prejudices of the logic of natural science, with the result that as the soul becomes an object for respectable scientific investigation, it also becomes an exclusive one. It inhabits astral worlds transcendental to the world of gross matter but experienced in terms of sensations, visions, yet of a more refined and more select sort. Thus, while most of them claim the right to be scientific, in actual fact their methods are not the best in science, while oddly enough, good science remains very incomplete with respect to its ideas concerning the soul, and though it has much to criticize it has little to add. Both sides are expressions of the same dilemma: the soul is everywhere yet nowhere; something like the Scarlet Pimpernel. The solution cannot come by peering to catch the elusive imp or by juggling with ideas. It involves the quest for a method at the point where the limits of the logically knowable have been reached. And this in turn presupposes a certain attitude and a certain spirit. We know that the soul is an everyday experience, yet we have no language to talk of it which is not vitiated by abuses of the language of reason or sense perceptions. The poverty of language means that the experience itself tends to be lived but partially and incompletely. This in turn leads to a whole series of disturbances and sufferings, the nature of which challenges our confidence in the methods of acquiring knowledge we have adopted and in the philosophies on which they have been built. Thus the quest for a method is not to be reserved to a few theoreticians. It involves the experience of the quest for a language and the anguish and the pain which accompany all attempts to give voice to that spirit in the depths of the soul which groans for expression and recognition. Culturally our civilisation has lost that naiveness which, in the past, enabled language to convey the fullness of the life of the soul. We lack the words because the old ones will not do the work for us. And yet it is not a matter of coining new words. So we resort to shaping and reshaping those we have into makeshift tools to express what we mean, but always *just not quite*. The use of words is not merely a question of definition: it belongs to the life and soul of him who uses them.

Thus, the psychologist caught by the spirit of the times seeks to be scientific or seeks to be philosophical, but at bottom he knows that these are makeshifts, mere approximations, imperfect translations into foreign logics of an experience that is its own logic. And the lack of a logic of the soul means that our age is full of the dread *(Angst)* of a soul, our age has lost the means of recognising and of expressing that soul. Possessing these means naively at first, it lost them as a result of the greater differentiation of mind from nature and the world around it. It follows that the rediscovery of a language of the soul involves more than a return to a naive, instinctive participation within it. It seems as though we are called upon to become conscious of the sort of "fact" the soul is, and this involves a very different situation from that concerning any other sorts of "facts". Yet to stand on the limits of the logically unknowable is an intolerable situation suffered as an irreconcilable tension that may or may not lead to the freeing of meaning and the resolution of conflicts. In order to characterise this vital confrontation with the limits of a world outlook, the frontiers of intellectual and perceptual vision, we suggest the word "pronoia" and call to mind that it was under this name that Athena was worshipped in Delphi, and the Virgin qualified in Christian hymnology.

Were this problem restricted to psychology we would have far more reserve to discuss it, but because we feel strongly that it is the problem of our age, that it has set its mark on all activities of our times, in art, music, the advanced sciences, in religion, philosophy, and logic itself, we consider it as constituting an important element in modern psychological thought. Pronoia, therefore, indicates the necessity for forethought before the mysteries of the unknowable at the same time as it indicates the need of coming to terms with it.

And in psychology particularly the role of pronoia is essential to an attitude that seeks to anticipate a process of development during which the entertainment of misleading expectations and inadequate presuppositions have a direct effect on the matter under investigation. In this respect what we have called the knowledge myth will have a strong appeal for psychology in so far as it maintains the hope that, given the analytic or synthetic methods, we will not only be able to explore the empirical mysteries of the soul but thereby have a basis for statements concerning psychic reality itself and its qualitative mysteries. Thus we will have dispensed with the need of taking into account from the very outset our scientific point of view and philosophical and religious considerations, both concerning problems of justification and those raised by the role of extra-mundane beliefs. We can proceed in the analysis of the soul as we have done in that of matter or mind. As this hope has already considerably affected modern theories of psychology, it will be necessary to discuss the knowledge myth in modern depth psychology and its practical application as psychotherapy. This criticism of the expectations raised by the advance of science is not to be understood then as a criticism of its methods in general, but rather of the inadequacy of our understanding of the limits of these methods when applied specifically to that mixture of empirical and qualitative mystery which is of the essence of the living soul. The criticism of the knowledge myth and the philosophy of science on which it is based is therefore indispensable if we are to place the young and enormously vigorous science of the soul on as firm and correct a foundation as is at present possible.

6: THE KNOWLEDGE MYTH IN PSYCHOLOGY

Towards the end of the XIXth century, Pierre Janet undertook the study of psychic automatisms on the basis of the analytic empirical method which he introduced as follows: "Les phénomènes les plus élevés et les plus importants sont loin d'être les plus simples; ils présentent au contraire bien des modifications, des développements accessoires qui empêchent de bien comprendre leur véritable nature. Les faits les plus élémentaires aussi bien en psychologie que dans les autres sciences, sont recherchés aujourd'hui de préférence, car on sait que leur connaissance plus facile à acquérir *eclaircira beaucoup celles des formes plus complexes.*" [7] The higher forms, such as volition, free will, and moral values are far too complex, and though they would appear to be the natural objects to study, as indeed they had been in the past for philosophy, nevertheless their complexity does not make them suitable for scientific investigation. Yet the hope is clearly formulated that these complex phenomena, though not so easy a subject for scientific investigation, will be better understood as a result of the knowledge acquired in more elementary fields.

Clearly, when Janet referred to free will, moral values, volition, as complex *facts*, he did not mean that they are facts like the gestures, grimaces, and general behaviour patterns, however complex, he was going to observe. Yet he referred to both as facts, and to both in terms of complex and simple. In such circumstances a confusion between volition and the acts of volition is bound to arise. Five hundred pages later we read, "Le génie, au contraire, est une puissance de synthèse capable de transformer des idées entièrement nouvelles qu'aucune science antérieure n'avait pu prévoir, c'est le dernier degré de la puissance morale. Les hommes ordinaires oscillent entre ces deux extrêmes, d'autant plus déterminés et automates que leur force morale est plus faible, d'autant plus dignes d'être considérés comme des êtres libres et moraux que la petite force qu'ils ont en eux et dont *nous ignorons la nature grandit davantage.*" [8]

Thus, on the one hand, this conclusion is in strict accordance with the best scientific tradition, and Janet keeps well within the legitimate limits of his method. On the other hand, we are not at all set at ease because this "little force" we know nothing of interests us greatly. If, after all, personality depends on this elusive unknown and we remain as ignorant of it at the beginning as we are at the end in spite of promises to the contrary, and if this little unknown is the force that moves mountains, that can make or destroy a civilisation, we feel somehow someone, somewhere, should be able to speak a language appropriate to it. Clearly, passing it to science from philosophy and back to philosophy from science is not going to get us very far. In this case, then, the knowledge myth takes the form of an expectation promoted by the confusion of logic, and maintained by the very real desire to know something about personality with which we start out, and the confession of ignorance with which we are forced to end up. Real discoveries and progress are weighed against disillusionment; the one emphasized, the other glossed over. We await a morrow that never arrives when indeed we should know what today has slipped through our fingers.

From the knowledge myth at the end of the XIXth century we pass to its appearance in the writings of Sigmund Freud inaugurating the XXth century. Here too, we must distinguish the definite factual premises of psycho-analysis as a science from the interpretations and expectations which go far beyond its legitimate empirical boundaries.

In Freud's writings a step of great consequence is noted: meaning was introduced into the more primitive phenomena of psychological behaviour. The more complex cultural forms can now at least be *explained* by the simpler psychological ones. What makes Freud fascinating to the empiricists and scientists is not so much the rather spectacular sexual theories, but the much deeper possibility that the missing link which will finally connect us to Jupiter's throne has been found. The higher forms purposely omitted by Janet in his empirical investigations of the more primitive psychic phenomena need no longer be left out; they can now appear in the material studied by the psychologist of the unconscious. A correlation can be established between them and the more primitive, *i.e. psychological* facts. Thus it is that in this sense the theory of sublimation offers to link meaningfully physiological facts to the *cultural* "facts" of the personality itself. It follows that the headache of philosophy and metaphysics is now got rid of. One has only to go to the primitive psychological causes to discover all the material from which the higher can be derived. If we concentrate long enough on this "discovery" we soon develop the myopia necessary to mistake it for the real thing. The similarities will be stressed and the dissimilarities discreetly passed over. The knowledge myth assumes such proportions, explanation so floods its legitimate boundaries, that calm philosophical exposition and clarification have to yield to apocalyptic threats of fire and damnation to cope with its insidious implications. That a whole generation should be caught and fascinated by material derived from the observation of pathological cases and used to provide the basis for a philosophy and an explanation of the highest spiritual and cultural values, cannot be explained merely as due to a confusion in logic or a reaction from the morality of a previous generation. Rather, it points to the drive behind the knowledge myth due to the intolerable tension that the separation of body and mind, spirit and nature, has produced.

Psychoanalysis in this sense owes its success to the fact that *in the theory of sublimation it offers a release from this tension and the fulfilment of the hope that we are at last on the way to the solution of the mystery.* But the theory of sublimation rests on the same old confusion. For, in so far as it explains by establishing a correlation between physiological behaviour and psychological or mental "phenomena", that is to say facts of the same order but far more complex, it has indeed a legitimate claim. But, morality, volition, free-will, and particularly spirit are not reducible to mental phenomena and psychological behaviour, unless we presuppose the philosophical credo that mental facts are kinds of physical events and no more. The ambiguity between the concept and the act has allowed us to believe that by explaining the latter we have explained the former. As John Wisdom puts it — "By deduction we may pass from statements of one type to statements of the same type but not from statements of one type to statements of another type. We can pass from logical statements to logical, from ethical to ethical, from matter-of-fact to matter-of-fact, from psychological matter-of-fact to psychological matter-of-fact . . . And we cannot pass, neither by deduction nor by induction, from statements of fact, whether about things or about words, to logical statements." [9] Yet the problem is not merely logical, not merely a question of definition. Behind the confusion of logic is the drive which feeds the myth and without which much of the excitement that belongs to the hopes of a final solution will disappear and carry with it a part of the incentive required to sustain scientific enquiry.

Thus the fact that modern philosophy has been able to reveal many of the logical confusions contained in the thought of the older metaphysicians does not mean that it has freed itself from the original drive behind the misleading logic as Ayer seems to think. For, when Ayer writing on Berkeley's idealism says Berkeley "declares that the existence of sensible qualities consists of their being perceived, he must not be understood as putting forward a factual thesis. What he is doing is to lay a convention".[10] Wisdom can rightly point out that Ayer is making one point at the expense of another. For, were it the case that Berkeley knew he was laying down but a convention of language it can be seriously doubted whether he would have written at all. It was precisely the conviction that he was indeed saying something valid about reality that kept him going. Conversely it seems that behind the scientific hope to explain the higher phenomena in terms of those more within reach of scientific methods lies the same philosophico-methaphysical preoccupation, namely, to understand the world of mind in terms applicable to the world of physical observable reality around us. And any psychology which claims to do this in matters of the soul appeals not to the scientist as Freud insisted, but to the philosopher behind the scientist. In such cases one cannot separate science from philosophy for both essentially condition one another.

The attempts then to get back to spirit or to get out into nature which form a powerful undercurrent throughout the work of scientist and philosopher is a direct consequence of the split between body and mind. Both philosophy and natural science are under the pressure of a drive which impels them to expend their energies towards the solution of problems that exist only because of the dichotomy. Modern thought is characterized by its growing consciousness of the importance of discovering the unifying principle as well as by its realization of the logical impossibility of this principle being discovered within the framework of the established orders of philosophy and science as they stand at present. To find such a principle we must take up a position prior to the separation of nature and spirit whether this separation is understood factually or conceptually. Moreover, since a unifying principle will have to say something about the world and also about the mind, the most likely place to find it will be the soul in so far as psychological reality seems to participate in both. In the case of psychology, then, most theories concerning human motivation and the problems of instinct and spirit are vitiated from the very beginning: firstly, by philosophical presuppositions which themselves are the outcome of the separation of spirit and nature, and secondly, by a failure to grasp both the importance of the effect of observation on what is observed (the empirical aspect) and the role played by the drive to justification, which cannot be dismissed with impunity as extra-scientific or merely philosophical.

Psychology is neither about the body and its functions nor is it about ideas and their interrelations and contents. The problems of being, the meaning of reality and its ultimate analysis are problems of philosophy and metaphysics. Psychology concerns itself primarily with the soul, and were the soul a metaphysical entity psychology would necessarily be limited to metaphysics. But as things stand the soul is not as transcendental, nor for that matter as biological, as either metaphysics or science would have us believe. On the one hand it is about life, about how people think, feel, behave, their problems and their ways, not about the organs and functions with which they do this. On the other hand it is also about spirit and the meaning of life to people and these meanings are not exhausted by a history or analysis of ideas. In fact the very effective existence of the enormous mystery literature in our times is eloquent proof of the reality of the soul irrespective of the validity or correctness of the mystico-philo-sophico-scientific theories concerning it. *And if the soul is an unknown that seems to elude our attempts to understand it, this is because we have as yet no language and no method appropriate to the phenomenology of its reality. It is not because we lack some special knowledge to be realized mystically or intuited by some special faculty; nor is it the case that by further neurological or biological discoveries we will resolve its empirical mystery as the knowledge myth would have us believe.*

The soul being a reality of its own, psychology must, therefore, be clear about the principles that define this reality, the methods to be employed in its investigation, and the problem of justification connected with any interference that must necessarily occur as a result of the application of the method. The soul is a mystery indeed, but this mystery is, on the one hand the mystery of nature which it is possible to explore scientifically, and on the other it is a mystery which has been the object of religion to experience qualitatively and to cultivate *(cultus)*. In the former case justification and results are expected in terms of intra-mundane goals and achievements, but in the latter, justification rests on extra-mundane goals, in terms of redemption and illumination. Both these aspects of the soul are essential to it, and psychological method and its principle must issue from both these realities if it is to remain true to its matter and not pay lip service to philosophy when it refers to the history and analysis of ideas or to science when it refers to the investigation and control of bio-physical nature. The knowledge myth, moreover, when it appears in psychology, leads us to entertain the hope that either science or philosophy as they are at present practised will lead us to understand better the mystery of the soul. The knowledge myth is based on a misleading use of logic which should be clarified and exposed in all its insidious and protean nature. Then we may realise that, as far as a logos of the soul is concerned, the principle of the soul is not only independent of all other principles of mind and body, but very probably contains the possibilities of the reunification of these into a higher and more essential unity than it has at present been possible to achieve in Western culture.

7: CONCLUSION

Science implies observation and controlled interference with events in the world; these in turn presuppose a method by means of which the facts observed are interpreted and organized. The principles of such methods are established by philosophy, logic and mathematics. In the case of the specific methods of knowledge evolved since the time of Newton and Descartes, the principles on which both philosophy and science have been erected suffer from an essential dichotomy that precludes the possibility of understanding psychological reality in its own right. Any reformulation of principles therefore that will enable us to investigate psychological realities implies an essential criticism of the methods of science and philosophy, in particular the analytic and synthetic methods.

These methods while adequate for the investigation of physical phenomena and ideational sequences are inadequate when applied to psychological realities because they cannot overcome the split between matter-of-fact and ideas; therefore they are effective only if we consider the soul either as a sort of bio-physical fact subject to biological laws, or as an expression of mental processes. Therefore psychologies based on such assumptions are vitiated from the start and ultimately depend on philosophical credos of which they are merely a onesided extension of science or of philosophy.

Any expectation based on the hope that the understanding of more elementary or primitive phenomena will clarify our understanding of such psychological facts as volition, consciousness, personality, and extra-mundane beliefs, is based on a misleading logic which is a part and parcel of the dichotomy which runs throughout these methods. Finally, the application of scientific method in the past necessitated the putting aside of problems of justification as extra-scientific and therefore proper only to ethics and religion. But in matters of the soul, this sort of scientific ethics is unacceptable in so far as interferences into the living process of the soul imply the possibility of definite influences that already predetermine the "matter" under investigation in such a way that it yields only what has already been projected into it. Moreover, the unknown which is the soul is as clearly different from the unknown in nature as it is from the unknown which is beyond nature; it seems to participate of both, yet is a qualitative whole in its own right. Thus the initial expectations in the fruitfulness of the methods employed to investigate this unknown are already a reflection of the philosophical credo on which these methods are based. In this respect then it is clear that if we do not put spirit in, we can hardly expect to get spirit out. And if we omit spirit we are unjust to the matter at hand in so far as the soul is as much qualified by spirit as it is by body.

These preconditions for an adequate science of the soul and its practical application as psychotherapy are closely interwoven with one another. The problem of justification, for instance, implies also an initial act of faith with respect to the method on the one hand and our "matter" on the other. The conditions governing the application of the method are to a certain extent created by the method itself; they arise objectively from the requirements of the "matter" for the investigation of which the method has been forged. But above all, the quest for an adequate method signifies a quest for a set of values of verification. By differentiating the soul from the body, we also thereby invalidate the criteria of truth and falsity as these apply to the sense-observable, phenomenal world. To understand therefore what is meant by psychological "facts" or psychological "realities", or to put it differently what is meant by psychological "experiences" as these impose themselves on a science of psychology, we must consider such problems of verification as will inevitably arise in conjunction with psychological events.

Chapters II, III, and IV, then will be concerned with the elucidation of this important aspect of any science of the soul.

That the soul needs to be formulated, given a voice, means that we are moving towards a rediscovery of its values *consciously* after having possessed them as a gift naively, and then lost them. This is undoubtedly the greatest spiritual adventure of our age and requires the mobilisation of all our powers and the realisation that *the cure of the soul is a far more universal problem than it appears to be when viewed within the context of the clinic or the psychotherapist's consulting room.* And, this fact can be overlooked neither by science nor philosphy; indeed, it would seem that one of the deepest sources of fulfilment and satisfaction of both these manifestations of the spirit is derived from their connection to the soul from which they have issued and to which they will ultimately address themselves.

1   Wittgenstein, L.: *Tractatus Logico-Philosophicus*, London, 1922, 6. 32.
2   Eddington, A. S.: *Space, Time and Gravitation*, Cambridge, 1921.
3   *op. cit.*
4   Bacon, F.: *Collected Works*, London, 1881, p. 3.
5   *op. cit.*, p. 33.
6   Mesmer, F.: *Mémoire sur la découverte du magnetisme*, Genève, 1779, p. vi. Translation in: *"Mesmerism" by Dr. Mesmer (1779) with an Introductory Monograph by Gilbert Frankau*, London, 1948, p. 28.
7   Janet, P.: *L'automatisme psychologique*, Paris, 1894, p. 1.
8   *op. cit.*, p. 478.
9   Wisdom, J.: *Philosophy and Psycho-analysis*, Oxford, 1953, p. 246.
10 Ayer, A. J., and Winch, R.: *British Empirical Philosophers*, London, 1953, p. 16.

CHAPTER II

1: PSYCHOLOGICAL EXPERIENCE

THE REALITY on which we can build a comprehensive, unifying logic of body and mind is the reality of the soul. But this reality is not so easily established. When Stout, for instance, defined psychology as "neither the study of a soul nor merely the study of human behaviour" but a matter of "psychical states and processes, their objects as such and the conditions of their occurrence" he was considering the soul as meaningful through its psychical states or experiences which are no different from mental states and experiences such as willing, feeling, perceiving, disliking, believing, wishing, etc. *The distinction between psychical states and psychological experience* which is analogous to the distinction between a physical object and its sense data, a proposition and the sentence expressing it, *is nowhere made in modern psychology*. On the contrary it is implicitly accepted that mental processes and psychological experience are one and the same thing. Thus Wisdom can write without expecting much criticism that: "In defining 'science' and 'mental facts' we shall arrive at a definition of 'psychology' because psychology is the science of mental facts." [1]

This confusion is a consequence of the separation of nature and spirit in the XVIth century in the wake of Greek philosophy, whose most serious omission is that it left no place for the soul in the scheme of things except as an expression of biological life force, or else as a mental process whose ultimate subject, if any, was transcendental and hence unknowable and undiscoverable by the new methods. Consequently, those who deal with psychology fall into three different classes: firstly, the empiricists for whom psychic processes could be known and investigated by the scientific methods of experimentation and generalisation of the data observed; secondly, the logicians and analytical philosophers for whom psychic processes are expressions of mind and form part of the general analysis of mind and the clarification of the various problems raised; and thirdly, the speculative and mystical philosophers for whom the psyche is a transcendental entity to be known by a series of reasonings and intuitions culminating in a sudden illumination, experience or vision, abstracted from the contingency of space, time and the body.

These are the methods of response of a conception of things that knows only the axioms of mathematics and logic, or the phenomena of sensible perceptions. It is not surprising, therefore, that the many modern psychologies are bound to distort psychological reality when they take for granted principles that are not in the least either absolute or final, and which if adequate for physical and logical reality are inadequate in the case of that reality which is of the soul.

On the other hand, the power of the logic of language to reduce the psychological fact to one of sensation or mentation cannot be regarded as due only to a cultural prejudice; we have to ask how it is that that prejudice acquires such a power of conviction in the first place. It must surely correspond to an objective reality, to the structure of things. In this connection it does seem a peculiar property of the soul to know and to experience itself through sensible perceptions and mentative processes. Hence when we seek to establish the reality of the soul we do not only come up against the cultural prejudices of a whole world outlook, we are not only handicapped by the language at our disposal, but furthermore, we are confronted with the specific logic of the soul itself, its peculiarly elusive yet nevertheless effective and real presence.

Now if the soul is not identical with perception nor with concepts, wishes, or other special mentative or so-called "psychic" processes, what more is it? Or rather, how are we to "look" at it at all? For, we look at material objects, perceive images, dreams, fantasies; but these of themselves are not the soul. Similarly we form ideas on which we can pass judgements of belief, disbelief, doubt, but we do not consider the soul as any one of these ideational processes. Indeed, at this point there is a tendency to construe the soul as the subject of the sum of all states of perception and mentation. But then if the term soul is used to cover the totality of such mental processes, or again the subject of these, this is a special use of the word and does not coincide with the very definite meaning it conveys in such phrases as "he is a man without a soul." For in that case we should mean that he has no mental processes or that he lacks a self to which they can be related, which is clearly not the meaning intended to be conveyed by the proposition in question. *The only word which may serve our purpose is the word "experience".* But here we must advance with caution, in so far as the concept of experience is as loaded with the logic of perceptions as with that of ideas. We talk of the experience of sensations, images, pain, as synonymous with the perception of these; in fact, William James can go so far as to formulate a psychological theory of the emotions by reducing emotional experience to the perception of visceral changes. Moreover, many philosophers describe the feelings they get from exercising their reason as an experience. Thus, intellectual insights, deductions, or intuitive generalisations are often so powerful that although they are derived from non-empirical premises they acquire an empirical character, not because of any empirical content but because of the power of the experience. Heidegger's concept of "Dasein" is an instance of such a philosophical process. The claim that philosophy is itself an experience, that the reality of its concepts is the fruit of the patient exercise of philosophical activity, does not answer the objection that the term experience tends to overflow its legitimate boundaries, to convey meanings that are not intended in the original conceptual premises. Indeed, such a confusion is understandable because of the lack of a logic of the soul. In the case described above, the word "experience" overflows its original contexts simply because it refers to something more than the perceiving or conceiving subject, when this is understood in the specific sense of the perceptor or activator of mental or material states. It refers to the soul. Thus, in psychological experience, both concepts and sensible perceptions are the sources of that experience, where the term "psychological experience" does not presuppose a perceiving or cognising subject (the subject of mental acts or states as wishing, willing, dreaming, imagining) but the subjects as soul. For if it referred to the subject in the first sense then the subject of psychological experience would be no different from a photographic plate or alternatively an exquisitely constructed calculating machine. We do not only register sensible perceptions when observing a landscape, we also *experience* them. Moreover, we not only formulate thoughts, but we can experience them. Now a sensible perception cannot be the object of a sensible perception, nor is a sensible perception the object of a concept: the object of $2+2=4$ is not the sensible perception of the marks "2", "+", "4", but the concept $2+2=4$. Moreover, it makes sense to talk of my experience of a red flag or the colour redness and it also makes sense to talk of my experience of triangularity, and this is not the same as saying that I perceive a red flag or that I hold the concept of triangularity before my mind.

Clearly then, the experiencing subject is neither a mind nor a body, for these cannot be the subjects of their own states nor can they be the subjects of each other's states. And therefore in this sense, it is appropriate to say that the soul is neither the thinking, willing, wishing subject nor is it the perceiving material body, but rather the experiencing subject. And if there is a sense in which the personal pronoun can be used to say I will, I wish, I think, or I perceive, there is also a sense in which it can be made to say *I experience and not mean that I am merely wishing, willing, thinking or perceiving. Once this distinction is accepted the soul ceases to be the mysterious subject of psycho-mental states beyond scientific enquiry; for psychological experience is an everyday fact, a phenomenon we know of and live by all along and therefore possible of examination and description.*

The subject as soul stands out distinctly from the subject as mind and the subject as body. Therefore, the existence of the soul is a fact, but a fact which is affirmed not through a distinct perception of a physical event or thing, nor is it affirmed by a rational series of moves culminating in a proof; it is a fact in its own right, either confirmed by itself as sensations confirm themselves, or not at all. But since the terms "experience", "fact" and any other equivalent words have suffered from a systematic loading in favour of a language of perception or of mentation, it will be necessary, in order to avoid confusion, to use such terms with the qualification of the adjective "psychological" to cover the order of psychological facts as distinct from physical or mental facts. The meaning will be built up from usage and its contexts.

In this sense of psychological factualness or reality, spirits may or may not exist, a pain may or may not be imaginary, a sensation may or may not correspond to a physical object, but all these are real in the sense that they can be experienced and this experience constitutes a world in its own right. It is just this property of ideas and objects to be the sources of an experience that is real and whose reality is not identical with that of mind or body that is the basis for talking of psychological facts and psychological selfhood in a significant manner. It follows, moreover, that there can be no observation and no thought which, however detached and objective, is not a possible source of psychological experience. We can never get away from the soul. Hence the notion of objectivity, impersonality or abstraction so dear to science is impossible when we introduce the experiencing soul into our picture of the cosmos since every abstraction is also the source of psychological experience. Thus the exclusion of psychological experience from systematic philosophical thought and scientific investigation does not do away with the soul. It persists underground, so to speak, sending up mysterious and disturbing effects. And the more systematic the exclusion the more mysterious and unreal appears the psychological fact to the point of view in question so that the soul itself tends to disappear beyond the horizons of the knowable.

Recognition of psychological factualness or reality releases us from the tension of trying to explain and get to the soul through the mind. It brings with it new hope and the possibility for a valid and original development. Just as the body grows and matures and just as it falls ill and medicine seeks to control, predict and understand its vicissitudes; just as the mind develops, enriching itself with philosophical and historical methods of analysis and synthesis; so too the soul has its own developmental processes leading to psychic maturity and psychic plenitude, intimately related to the other two but not reducible to them. And if the soul in the past had been the main concern of religion, there is no doubt that today psychology seeks to understand and can understand the soul, its health and its sickness, provided it respects the facts which religion respected. For the difference between religion and psychology in this sense is one of form, and not of content. The priest turns to psychology when he seeks to understand the soul in its totality, and the psychologist turns to the contents of religion, not its presuppositions, for the same purpose.

Now, as we have seen, the recognition of an independent psychological reality creates the need for a new method and principles of verification. But, since truth and falsity are closely connected to the use of the concepts of reality and unreality, it follows that the acceptance of psychological factualness brings about a feeling of a loss of reality, in so far as we have been trained to acknowledge as *real*, physical facts on the one hand and mental facts on the other. And as the point of view of psychology is based upon living experience, it follows that the passage to a world outlook that takes the soul into account will involve, in addition to methodological and logical difficulties, those raised by the *experience* of these. For as philosophy seeks desperately for its reality values so the soul passes through a corresponding phase of despair and unreality brought about by the loss of values it had learned to depend upon for good or for bad. Psychology in philosophy and in science is therefore a real experience and a necessary adventure.

The quest for reality values in psychology as we have described it involves two different phases: firstly, the establishment of psychological factualness or psychological reality as a reality common to all and experienceable by all, that is to say, its general empiricism; and secondly, the conditions of verification *within* this empiricism. Verification in the latter sense seeks to establish the criteria that govern the relational predicates "is true", "is false": it tells us under what conditions we can say so-and-so is true and such-and-such is false. For if in one sense all psychological experience is true by definition, like every historical fact is true, such facts are useless to science, whose truth values flow from systematic interpretations with a view to verification by prediction.

In the following section we will try to show that psychology is no different in the principles establishing the factualness or reality of the soul than the analogous process in science and philosophy with respect to matter and mind. For, *just as we do not perceive matter but only material things, and just as we cannot conceive of mind but only of mental events, so too, we do not experience or verify the existence of the soul directly but only through psychological experiences.* With the reality of the soul established, it will then be possible to deal in greater detail with the problems of verification proper to a study of psychological processes, and the method of science most adequate to them.

2: REALITY IN SCIENCE AND PHILOSOPHY

"L'expérience est la source unique de la vérité: elle seule peut nous apprendre quelque chose de nouveau; elle seule peut nous donner la certitude".[2] Poincaré wrote these words at the turn of this century, two hundred years and more after Bacon's similar statements. Experience is a matter of verification through sensible perceptions; such verification carries with it the conviction of a certainty which belongs not to any intrinsic quality proper to physical objects but as a property of the relationships that obtain among them. Science is the study and the discovery of these relationships which, with the help of the laws of logic and mathematics, enable us in turn to make further statements confirmable, however, by looking at the world, that is to say, by the senses. Thus the world of the scientist is the world of matter-of-fact, and he arrives at an understanding of this world through the reality and the effectiveness of the mind's power of cognition. We shall refer to the former aspect of science as the reality of sensible perceptions or matters-of-fact and to the latter as the logic of ideas. Certainty and truth in science then belong to the logic of ideas, but the reality of this truth depends ultimately on that of matters-of-fact. Now, in so far as philosophy also concerns itself with the logic of ideas it plays an important role in science, but strictly speaking nothing is scientific unless it can be verified through sense-experience. Therefore, in philosophy, the presence of the certainty of logical proofs is offset by the impossibility of relating their contents to experience, or at least to some sort of experience. At most the philosopher has no choice but to affirm that the reality of mind is ultimately a transcendental reality, a spiritual substance, or else, that the reality of mind derives from the reality of matters-of-fact, in so far as ideas, too, are matters-of-fact occurring in this world to a specific spatio-temporal brain. Neither of these statements however conveys the conviction and hence, reality values, attached to the statements of science. And as it is from this centre that science and philosophy unfold and it is to this point that they ever return, it will therefore be necessary to examine the nature of reality in science and in philosophy a little more closely.

The Reality of Sensible Perceptions

Science does not specifically affirm the reality of the world; the meaning of such affirmations is a matter for philosophy to settle. Science is quite content to work on the world as that which happens to be at hand. To this purpose it has developed a set of rules and an ethics which is characterised by its systematic exclusion of everything which is not pure observation, that is, sensible-perception. As Russell says — "The kernel of the scientific outlook is the refusal to regard our own desires, tastes, and interests as affording a key to the understanding of the world." [3] The ethics of the scientist, his credo, is his disinterested ethical neutrality towards the world which he perceives through his senses. The understanding he so acquires refers by definition to the world of matters-of-fact. Hence the world Russell intends is no more than the world of physics whose reality the scientist takes for granted. The question we therefore ask ourselves is not what philosophical meaning we are to give to reality, but the far more relevant yet simpler question, what property of the sensible world is it that enables science to consider its world as real?

If there is no specific observable experience that as far as scientific proof is concerned can prove that this world is real, there is however one aspect of empiricism that characterises matters-of-fact in relation to reality, that the world of sensible perceptions is shared or can be shared by all alike. To the extent that I predict on the basis of a scientific theory that this or that event will occur at such and such a time, and that I alone will be able to observe it, to that extent my scientific theory lacks conviction, and my observation, reality value. It is important to point out that this

aspect of empiricism which characterises matters-of-fact, while determining the reality values of such a world, is not thereby in any sense
an absolute or sufficient property of reality nor is it a definition. The
problem of a definition of reality is, as we have seen, a matter for philosophy.

As a result of the correlation that obtains between the concept of
reality and the fact that an event can be shared by all, the scientist expects
the sun to rise tomorrow, he looks for it in the east and not in the north,
and he tends to believe honest Jones when he says that he saw a falling
star on the night of the presidential elections; but he tends to disbelieve
him if honest Jones says that he saw three full moons on that same night.
It is clear that, while such tendencies to belief and disbelief are governed
by our knowledge of the world based on high type generalisations, it is
also clear that they are governed by an act of faith that springs directly
from a *consensus gentium*. For, if a whole nation for fifty years claimed
to perceive three full moons in the sky, science, in spite of its knowledge
of the number of planetary bodies in the proximity of the earth, would be
far less willing to reject such evidence and would be persuaded to examine
its foundations in reality more closely.

The difference between the example of the three moons and the reality
of the world of science is a matter of statistical frequency. The world
of the scientist is the world as it has been observed and shared by the
majority for an undetermined period of time. If one part of the world
ceases to share the sense perceptions of the rest and if this continues for a
long period of time, it will certainly affect the reality value of the world as
science sees it. But if *any* person entering that region of the world also
shares the perceptions of its occupants, then science cannot but accept
as real the objects of these perceptions: *the criterion of reality in this sense
is that the perception can be shared.* Whether or not these perceptions
coincide with the predictions of a scientific theory and hence are true
relative to that theory is not the meaning of truth or reality we are here
discussing. Moreover the property of being shareable by all should be
distinguished from the idea of collective truths. In this sense the evidence
of one man may be scientifically more true than the evidence of a crowd
under hypnosis; but then such evidence rests on the presupposition that
it would have been shared by others in that person's position. Knowing
what to expect, or what it would be like if one were there to register the
perception is another way of expressing the principle of reality underlying the sense-perceptible world as shared or shareable by all alike.

It looks, therefore, as though the world of the scientist and that of
the common man is fundamentally the same. Any difference between them
is but a matter of degree. The scientist possesses both a greater knowledge
of generalisations and rules, and sensitive machines to extend the range of
his sensible perceptions, such as lenses, vibrating wires, photographic plates.
In both cases generalisations about the world and about the future course

of events are confirmable by sense-experience. Scientific statements therefore will be just as valid for the world of the common man as they are for science.

But on closer examination, the world of the scientist and that of the common man differ in one fundamental respect: the common man never makes the original act of faith which characterises the scientist of abstracting from his field of vision subjective feelings, desires, or interests. The common man participates in the world as a whole and not only through his senses; and this world is qualitatively different from its parts. Now, the scientist *qua* scientist by an explicit act of abstraction participates in the world only through one of its aspects, namely, its sensible reality and the relations that obtain in that reality which he formulates with the aid of his mind. It follows, therefore, that he has still to show whether it will at all be possible to pass from statements concerning this cross section of reality to statements concerning that whole which is the basis of the common man's view of reality. Nowhere is there more confusion and more ambiguity. For on closer examination the result is that science is not in fact affirming anything about the world common to man but only about one aspect of that world which by its exclusive and one-sided development it tends so to emphasize that it canalises collective experience into a misleading logic and a distorted picture of even the commonest realities. Thus, when Russell talks of the scientist understanding the world he can only mean by definition the world of sensible perceptions and the relations that obtain between them. Yet it is quite evident that the concept of the world does and should include for the common man his passions, desires and interests.

The world, therefore, as it is experienced by the common man is not the world as it is formulated and seen by science. The scientific man is an abstraction not a reality. Yet if this abstraction is convenient to the scientist in that it permits him to proceed with his investigations without concerning himself with such non-scientific problems, his attitude is not sufficiently justified by this appeal to a principle of utility or convenience. Behind the ambiguity we can discern the knowledge myth binding the scientist to the misleading idea that he is saying something of the world as a whole, and the common man to the expectation that the results achieved in the part will illuminate and clarify this whole. But the physis of the scientist is, as we have seen, by his own definition, a physis created by a philosophical act that separates and abstracts reality into mind on the one hand and body on the other; while the physis of the common man is based on no such presupposition but presents itself as a whole that includes much that science and philosophy have seen fit to exclude. And while they have repeatedly expressed the hope that it is possible to pass from the one to the other, from the more primitive, elementary or simple to the more complex, they have still to show us how this is to be achieved when the complex happens to be a qualitative whole different from its parts.

By its refinement and elaboration of the possibilities of the world of sensible perceptions and mathematical relations, science has given a definite meaning to reality as it is expressible in such concepts as "facts", "empirical", "nature", "physis", "world", "cosmos", or their equivalents. In so doing science tends to ignore the possibility that a "thing" can be fact and hence real in the sense that it is shared and shareable by all alike, and consequently a part of the world, of nature, *and yet not be based on an observation of the world as it is knowable through acquaintance by means of sense perception.* However, because of the enormous progress of science we have lost sight of its humble origins and its guiding principles to the extent that we can hardly imagine that a non-scientific reality exists. Yet it is clear that there is no contradiction in maintaining the possibility of a field or reality other than that defined by any one specific scientific point of view. It is not reality that is defined by science but science that must seek out reality. When the relativity of science is lost sight of, therefore, and when its truth values are taken as absolutes, reality and the world are only too easily straightjacketed into the categories of a specific outlook to the exclusion of all other possibilities. Of course, modern thought never really expresses itself in such a crude formula as reductionism; nor does it admit that its world outlook and its evaluation of reality is exclusively or absolutely scientific in the sense in which "scientific" refers to the reality of matters-of-fact merely. It prefers to regard the issue as one of comparison and ultimate synthesis of the various major orientations to reality. Such a synthesis, moreover, is postulated as being explicitly a synthesis of the human being, who thus affords us the principle of unification of the various outlooks. Thus, humanism regards such expressions of the spirit as science, art, philosophy, and religion as equally valid multi-faceted aspects of one reality. But this attempt at unification forgets two things of importance: firstly, that any such unifying principle presupposes a language and a method that is not derived from any one of its sub-classes; and, secondly, that any principle which will unite the various branches of human knowledge and experience must not only be posterior to them but certainly prior to them. Moreover, humanism assumes that the expressions of human interest are unified by the general concept of the human spirit, which, though divided in its various expressions, is one in its essence. If this were so then this essential unity of the human spirit should be able to express itself over and above the diversity of its expressions: it should not only be a formula, it should also be a *fact*. But the moment humanism is established as a fact the human spirit comes into conflict and opposition with non-human energies, whether of a natural or a supernatural order. Humanism in this general sense is, of itself, inadequate to unify on an empirical basis the various expressions of spirit and has led to the crisis of makeshifts and ineffective syntheses as a defence against the dangers that threaten the unity of modern values. The characteristic common to all these points of view is the possibility of including the whole in the part. And although this process is relatively legitimate, as, for instance, when art formulates pictures of the wholeness of the world and of man, or, when philosophy builds systematic pictures of the wholeness of reality, judgements within these points of view are not to be taken as referring to wholeness in any general sense. We are misled when we allow our vision to be closed in by the horizons of this part-view and so come to believe that the whole expressed in this way is an expression of the wholeness itself which is over and above its parts and is the principle of unity of all reality and, therefore, that the validity of judgements referring to the one can be carried over to the other.

In this respect science is most open to this error: having discovered and established a method of its own based on a general principle of what is and is not explorable by this method, it then proceeds again and again to formulate the expectation that it is on the way to a better understanding of reality where the meaning of reality overflows the clearly defined and legitimate limits set by the principles of the method and its original outlook. We shall see later on that science anticipates but does not itself express the principle of unity of reality which remains in this respect a spirit and an empiricism in its own right.

The Reality of Ideas

The use of the term "mind" to cover such processes as wishing, feeling, believing, hoping, loving, and thinking presents a difficulty characteristic of the body-mind dichotomy. For while such processes together with memory, hallucinations, visions, dreams, can be regarded as differing from the typical behaviour of material objects and therefore not predicable of matter, they can nevertheless be regarded as properties of a *kind* of matter. Thus the reality of mind would be derived from and depend upon the reality of matter. Conversely, by the same stretch of logic, philosophy can extend the use of the term "mind" to cover the immediate object of a perception so that in this sense of the term we never really perceive material objects, only their sense impressions or sense data. From this point of view, even sense perception is a mental activity and must be regarded as a property of a non-material substance referred to as mind or psyche. Whether the original source of sense impressions is material or mental is not germane to our subject. What is of importance is to notice that the term "mind" is used also to signify in particular the possibilities of conception or cognition. In this sense of mind such things as memory, dreams, wishes, feelings, fears, hopes, beliefs, are considered as states of mind and not of body because they are recognised only by being expressed. An animal cannot wish, it cannot even for that matter desire anything, unless we attribute to it the possession of a mind by means of which it can formulate a desire or a wish. Thus, while undoubtedly animals must have a mind with which to perceive and register sense impressions, primitive feelings, and to regulate and coordinate their physical processes, we hesitate to attribute minds to them because of this ambiguity of the term "mind". For, while the powers for highly coordinated teleological actions, for experiencing sorrow, happiness, love, and like manifestations can be explained on a purely mechanical behaviouristic hypothesis, for instance, the conditioned reflex, the term "mind" is also used to cover a very different property which no animal has yet shown, and that is the power of conception, the power to use language in a *meaningful* way. The attempt of behaviourism to translate even the use of language into behaviouristic series of acts fails because, as Broad clearly argued, it makes sense to ask of a series of complicated acts whether they are intelligent or merely automatic. Thus animals whose behaviour is similar to human behaviour motivated by desire, or wishes, or guided by volition, are nevertheless not spoken of in the same way, however close the analogy. In one sense the possession of a mind seems to imply a plasticity of response, a capacity to influence and to change material events that defies all the laws of connection as they appear in a strictly deterministic material world. And this capacity is inseparable from the capacity for conception. Without conception, without the power to formulate ideas it is hardly conceivable that mind can influence or detach itself from the material world on the one hand, and from the inner world of image stimuli on the other. Without conception, for instance, man would be at the mercy of stimuli as they came. And that we should call this condition "mental", however non-physical the stimulus and the medium in which it is received, clearly is not the use of the term "mind" that is fundamental or characteristic of its meaning. It is only where there is the possibility to say, "I am afraid", "I desire", or again, "there is fear" or "there is desire", that we are inclined to affirm the presence of mind.

Yet this basic aspect of mind does not satisfactorily cover the world of experience as the philosopher conceives it. For, while he can ascribe reality to the mind, and while he need not refer to matter as the source of that reality, he has nevertheless no immediate proof and no possibility of reference as to the ultimate nature of this reality. The reality of mind for the philosopher is not given to him by any *a priori* proposition or special illuminative insight but is based on the existence of conception in much the same way as the reality of matter for science is based on the possibility of sense perception. Conception cannot therefore be defined just as vision cannot be defined; it is either known by personal possession or not at all. The reality of the world of ideas is ultimately reducible also to the fact that it is shared or shareable by all alike. He who says that $2+2=5$ has something wrong with him as he who says he saw three full moons on the night of the presidential elections. But, unlike the world of matters-of-fact, if a whole nation were to believe that $2+2=5$ then we would not doubt the structure of the picture of reality present to us, but only tend to assume that the mathematical or logical conventions of this nation are different from ours. *The world of ideas tends to be absolute in a way the world of matters-of-facts can never be.*

During the major part of the history of philosophy this absoluteness was believed to stem from the existence of a world of archetypes, as real if not more real than the world around us. And it was to this world that the term "mind" was often referred. Thus mind represents in this sense another world over and above the world of Physis, in which ideas subsist as physical objects exist in this world. Modern philosophy has shown that this "mind" is a projection of a logical property rather than the affirmation of an ontological reality. The absoluteness, eternity, and changelessness of ideas is a projection of their formal properties and not something that belongs to a state of being as physical objects can be said to belong to the world. The force of this argument is such that much of the old metaphysics can be seen to be based on this misleading use of logic and hence to have created a pseudo-world of transcendental realities that in fact exists only in the mind of those *conceiving* it. Any reality that such thought possesses is due to the reality of conception and of thought but to nothing else.

Thus, in spite of the absolute and transcendental character of ideas the reality of mind is ultimately not a matter of such speculations but is derived from the same source as that of the material universe, namely, the fact that everyone thinks and that their thought whenever it takes place shows the same structure and formal properties.

The philosopher is characterised by the fact, therefore, that he tends to emphasize this aspect of reality to the exclusion of any other. And, moreover, like the scientist it would seem that the philosopher is not distorting the world as it is known and experienced by the common man, but simply developing one of its possibilities. Philosophical conclusions therefore should be as valid for the common man as they are for the philosopher.

But this would be true only if the philosopher can show us how to pass from conception to that experience of reality as a whole which characterises the point of view of the common man. For here again the whole is different to its parts, and conception, however much it can be made to cover all mental acts or states, remains but one aspect of that qualitative whole of which sensible perceptions are another. To refer to this whole also as Mind is to be guilty of the same error as materialism when it refers to it as Matter, that is to say, it is to use the terms to cover meanings not originally contained by their definition, or else to use them in such a wide and general sense that they lose their effectiveness.

It follows that philosophy running parallel with science has tipped the scales the other way and has oriented the meaning of reality to cover the world of conception which then colours and distorts the meaning of such terms as "being", "fact", "experience", "mind", "soul", accordingly.

The unity and totality of the world of the philosopher, of the world of the mind, issues from the unity of conception and is a reflection of this progress and is not to be mistaken as the unity of that whole of which conception itself is a part. Thus, although everything can be included and covered by conception such as feelings, passions, desires, hopes and fears, this unity is not the same as that belonging to that generic whole of which these are so many aspects. By his exclusive preoccupation with mind by means of mind, the philosopher tends to forget that there can be non-physical realities that are shared or shareable by all alike and yet that do not belong to the logic of mind as such. The experience of desire, the experience of aesthetic judgements, of feelings, hopes and fears as well as the experience of all the various forms of conception cannot be regarded as so many more concepts or so many more physical events. As we have seen above we must clearly distinguish between the contents of mind and body and the possibility of the experience of these, a possibility which we referred to as due to the existence of the soul.

Thus, although the reality of mind and the reality of sensible perceptions and their objects establishes the world as historical fact and as idea, we nevertheless realise that this does not exhaust reality because of the possibility of psychological experience.

Philosophers may object to the above arguments on the grounds that reality has been reduced to a mere psychologism or a mere subjectivism and has been deprived of its objective character. But it must be pointed out that were reality the property of an ultimate mind this mind would be incomplete did it not also possess a soul. And since it makes sense to ask whether an all knowing Mind is also in possession of a soul, it follows that the terms "soul" or "psyche" are not synonymous with that of "mind" as so many philosophers and psychologists seem to have considered them.

Conversely the empirical scientist tends to regard soul as the expression of a life force which though irrational is nevertheless no more than the expression of bio-physical processess. But here again it does make sense to ask whether all biological processes imply a soul or not; it does make sense, for instance, to ask whether an amoeba has a soul. It is not at all clear that all life is necessarily an expression of soul, hence it is not clear that the term "soul" is but another way of expressing the quality of bio-physical processes.[4]

The fact is that the soul is both a mystery and a reality and that we cannot get very far unless we are prepared to accept it in both these aspects however paradoxical they may appear to be. Indeed the difficulty of accepting the paradoxical quality of reality as it presents itself to us in the case of the soul seems to be due precisely to this one-sided development of philosophy and science in favour of the mind and the body respectively and at the expense of the wholeness of experience. For neither the mind nor the body are in themselves paradoxical. Thus, by an act of faith missing in the original paradoxical yet qualitatively homogenous experience of reality that is the basis of the experience of that qualitative whole body-mind-soul, which is proper to the common man, science and philosophy have substituted a picture of reality that is indefinitely extendible, non-paradoxical, but incomplete. It remains to be seen therefore whether psychological reality, due to the existence of psychological experience, cannot provide us with that principle of unity and totality that the others have failed to do.

3: REALITY OF PSYCHOLOGICAL EXPERIENCE

It is not sufficient to formulate a description of psychological experience; it is necessary to affirm its reality as a basis for the application of a method and a theory as would for instance be required in psychotherapy.

In the last section we saw that the reality of science was based on sensible perceptions as that of philosophy and metaphysics is based on conception. We stressed the point that one of the distinguishing factors of the realities they deal with is that both sensible perception and conception are shared or shareable by all alike. Reality belongs less to the object as such than to the possibility of its being conceived or perceived by whoever crosses its field. Thus, if a person is witnessing a hallucination we tend to deny that he is perceiving a physical object but not to deny that hallucinations do as a matter of fact take place. In such cases we tend to talk of *different orders of facts, of different realities.* This shows that both science and philosophy possess effective criteria for the different orders of reality. They never say that such-and-such is real because it is a physical object or because it is a concept, only, that a thing is a concept or a physical object when it obeys the laws that obtain in these respective fields or orders of reality. In general these orders fall under two main headings, private and public, or subjective and objective. Trees, people, stars, as seen in dreams, hallucinations, or fantasies, are private "objects" of sensible perceptions, while trees, people, stars, as seen in waking life, are public "objects" of sensible perception. Similarly, the truths of mathematics and logic are public while delusional apperceptions are private conceptions. In one sense of reality, public reality is no less real than private, but in another sense public reality is more real, in that existence can be predicated of it without reference to the perceiving subject provided it is understood that if a subject existed at the moment and the time in question then it would be possible to perceive or conceive the reality in question. The latter interpretation is the meaning covered by the expression "sense of reality" to which we shall have occasion to return. But in both cases of the use of the term "reality" the ultimate criterion depends on affirmation by means of sensible perception and of conception.

Now psychological experience is real in precisely the same way. It is common to all, shared or shareable by all, and it is both public and private, each order being distinguished by the laws that obtain in their respective domains. The psychological experience of being in love is possible to all, it is a public reality, but the way I am in love, or the specific way some people experience the soul of love is subjective, that is to say private. The way Bluebeard loved his victims is peculiar to Bluebeard, but if a large class of people all loved the way Bluebeard loved and if this way of loving began to manifest itself generation after generation the subjectivity and peculiarity of this experience of love would tend to become public and objective. Thus, if the subject of psychological experience is the soul as distinct from the body or the mind, there is also an objective order of psychological realities corresponding to physical objects in the material world and to concepts in the mental. *This public reality of psychological experience is the basis for a science of the soul* that will not be a pure subjectivism or psychologism.

In matters of the soul there has long since been a recognised objective or public reality of psychological experience on the basis of which interpretations, judgements, expectations and predictions of a general, valid and hence objective or public character can be entertained. When for instance a writer describes the power and personality of a political leader he expects to be understood by his readers in this sense, that when they ever have the occasion to be in the presence of this personality they, too, shall "feel", "experience", that power and thus verify its reality. Moreover, he does not expect confirmation of his descriptions by someone taking a machine to register the pulse and measure the emanations from the body of that personality, nor does he expect a logician or a philosopher to question him and measure his intelligence quotient or his range of conceptual power.

In the field of religious experience, for instance, it takes much more than visions to sanctify a person, authenticated though they may be. Much more is required to establish the sanctity of his soul. But the fact that they can contribute, the fact that a person's soul can be regarded as more pure than another's, indicates that there have been and still are criteria of verification of a public order that do not depend on instruments to register the "facts" or on concepts to define them.

At this point it may be argued that what psychological experience is about is feeling judgments or judgments of value whether of a religious or non-religious order as opposed to scientific quantitative analyses and logical clarifications. This, however, is clearly not the sense in which the term "psychological experience" is here being used because the soul is much larger than the specific class of judgments of religious or other values, just as the mind includes much more than conceptual definitions and logical analyses. Judgments of value, feelings, emotions, do not exhaust the meaning of psychological experience though they are essential constituents of that experience.

The world of the psychologist, the world, that is to say, of the soul and of psychological experience is therefore real in the sense that it is shared or shareable by all alike — but not in the sense that it refers to or is defined by the physical event or by concepts or by a combination of both. Moreover, in so far as a psychological experience is public we shall refer to it as a psychological fact, and in so far as it is being experienced by a self we shall retain the term "psychological experience".

Now it follows that just as science by applying itself exclusively to the observation of sensible perceptions and philosophy to that of ideas gave a specific meaning to such terms as "fact", "experience", "reality", "existence", and thereby loaded the wholeness of reality with the logic of body or mind, so too, psychology in so far as it claims to deal with psychological realities and differentiates these from its other aspects will necessarily tend to modify our experience of reality in favour of the things of the soul. However, we will see that, unlike the physicalism of science or the conceptualism of philosophy, psychology as we understand it does no injustice to the mind or the body as these have done to the soul. This is because psychological experience issues from, and expresses itself through, both body and mind; therefore, by definition, it necessarily includes both in its orientation to reality and its experience as totality.

Indeed, the act of faith on which psychological method depends corresponds much more closely to the experience of the common man and requires no original act of abstraction and selection as do science and philosophy. The principles on which the logos of the soul is established neither narrows nor delimits its field of vision to the exclusion of others, because whatever we perceive, do, or think, is also a subject of psychological experience and hence a constituent of its reality. Psychological experience stares us in the face, to borrow a comparison of Jung's, in much the same way as the sun spots stared at the Schoolmen through Galileo's telescope.

If the differentiation of psychological experience and the affirmation of its reality correspond by analogy to the same process as takes place in science where the objects of sensible perception are also constituents of the reality of the physical universe and the objects of conception are constituents of the reality of mind, we are left with that intermediate field the reality of which though it cannot be denied in any ultimate sense nevertheless is not the same as those intended by objects of science or philosophy, namely, the private subjective world of imagination, visions, dreams, and apperceptions. We have already seen that this field of representations has been generally referred to as mind or as matter, or again, optionally, as psyche according to the specific orientation of the point of view in question. But as the expression "sense of reality" makes a clear distinction between this world and the world of physical objects or concepts common to and shareable by all, we must take this factor into consideration and irrespective of philosophical theory account for it by a suitable convention of reference. Thus we shall refer to the private world present to a perceiving, conceiving subject as the world of the psychoid, or mentoid, or physoid, according to whichever aspect we seek to emphasize at the moment; while the objective references of this world and its corresponding sense of reality we shall refer to as Body or Mind as the case may be. Now psychological experience corresponds in reality value to that which belongs in general to the expression "sense of reality" and not to that which corresponds to the relative and subjective realities of the private psychoid or mentoid worlds. Therefore the registration of a dream or fantasy by a perceiving conciousness must not be confused with the very different meaning and reality value of the psychological experience: psychological facts are real and the soul is real in the same sense as physical objects (Body) are real, or ideas (Mind) are real, but not in the sense in which hallucinations and dreams and fantasies and private conceptual combinations are real. Thus in this latter world I can ride broomsticks, see flying horses, perceive the Loch Ness monster, construct private meta-physical systems, and generally behave in a topsy-turvy way without necessarily implying that I have thereby experienced the psychological meaning of these adventures.

Thus the concept of the reality of the soul is not formed from the existence of such facts as dreams, fantasies, or the parapsychological pheno-mena of mind reading and telepathy, as these contrast with such realities as walking, talking, remembering, thinking. The concept of the soul is a *class concept* characterising the class of psychological experiences in much the same manner as matter and mind are class concepts covering the class of material things and mental events. On the other hand, the world of the psychoid or mentoid can be the source of psychological experiences as it can also metaphorically express such experiences. That is why Jung can say of fantasy: "For the important thing is not to interpret and understand the fantasies, but primarily to *experience* them". And con-versely: "All the works of man have their origin in creative imagination ... The creative activity of imagination frees man from his bondage to the 'nothing but'." [5] But this is in no way to assign to this intermediate world a privileged position with respect to the soul; on the contrary it is rather by reason of, and on the same level as, psychological experience occurring with respect to the realities of the world as perceived and conceived objectively and outside us that the private world of dream, fantasy and imagination can claim psychological validity. Hence Jung can add that "we *experience* various effects: from 'outside' by way of the senses, from 'inside' by way of fantasy".[6] Thus, although psychological experience and its reality are a qualitative and homogenous whole, we can refer to it under three separate headings according to whether it comes from or expresses itself through the physical world or Body, the mental world or Mind and the intermediate and neutral world of the psychoid or mentoid images.[7]

According to this point of view, a person with a very rich fantasy life may be very poor in actual value of psychological experience, and it would not be amiss to say that he has a poor or weak soul; conversely, a rich and deep soul may lead a very poor fantasy life. Alternatively, a person who has led a most active outer life and has had great success and much adventure need not necessarily be considered as psychologically rich in corresponding values: the quality and depth of his soul life may not have kept up with his outer activities. Furthermore, a person who has spent his life in a cell may have enriched and deepened his soul and this would not mean moreover that he has spent his time accumulating fantasies or writing learned treatises.

It will be seen, therefore, that psychological methods that have taken as their field of investigation the mentoid world whether defined as mind or physical imagery, whether investigated as a brain registering sensations and subject to laws, or a mind with its own laws of association, have failed to grasp the significance and all-comprising wholeness of psychological experience as a reality of its own. Such psychologies are guilty of much the same sin as science and philosophy when they equate their field of vision with the totality of experience as it presents itself to the common man. Empirical psychology and the psychology of intelligence in no wise permit us to pass from statements concerning the soul as a unique and qualitatively whole reality. In this connection psychological experience as here understood alone permits us to say that we are dealing with the soul as a whole and as a reality, and not with some one aspect of it abstracted and isolated for study by methods devised to investigate the world of matter or that of mind.

Thus the differentiation of psychological experience, the affirmation of its reality, enables us to entertain the hope that this reality is possible of description, as well as responsive to investigation, cultivation and verification. Yet the methods appropriate to this task may not correspond to those that have proved their value in quantitative measurement and logical analysis, but will have to be created by an incorporation of these into a logic and an empiricism qualitatively different from anything science and philosophy in their present unrevised form are able to produce.

The problem of method and the verification of psychological realities will therefore occupy us in the following chapter. As a result it will be seen that psychotherapy is but a particular application of the principles of a logos of the soul in terms of the meaning of life and spirit as they qualify, impinge upon, and express the universal and real values of psychological experience.

4: CONCLUSION

The object of psychology is properly speaking psychological experience. But psychological experience is derived from several sources: firstly, from the world of mind where we intend by "mind" processes of conception or ideation as a whole and their objects — desires, feelings, mathematical propositions, wishes, volition, and so forth; secondly, from that of body where we intend by "body" the objects of sensible perceptions. Intermediate to these realities stands the two dimensional world of dreams, visions, or private conceptual constructions, on the one hand, and sense data on the other, where there is no need to go beyond the representation immediately present to a perceiving consciousness to establish their realities. Now some philosophers and scientists have referred to this world as the world of mind or psyche and others have referred to it merely as another sort of body. As far as we are concerned this terminology gives rise to a considerable amount of confusion with respect to the meaning of reality; a philosopher or a scientist can talk of mind and mean either the datum immediately present to consciousness or else the class of realities, of concepts, or ideas. The same ambiguity applies to the use of the term "body" or "physical world". And as the passage from the one world to the other is also a passage from one meaning of reality to another and as the meaning of the reality of the soul is not at all clear or self evident, it follows that a clear distinction must be made between these various factors. Thus psychological reality belongs to psychological experience which in turn is not equivalent to the intermediate realm of the immediately given but rather to the objective reality of the soul, in much the same way as physical objects and concepts are objective and real. This intermediate world will be referred to as psychoid or mentoid indicating thereby that of itself it is not to be confused with the objective reality of the mind or of psychological experience.

These distinctions having been made and the reality of the soul established not in any ultimate sense but only in the sense of that which is given, which is at hand, much as matter is at hand for science and mind is at hand for the philosopher, we are able to express the hope of establishing a practice of and formulating a theory of psychological realities that will help us to understand better the soul's mystery and its actuality.

---

[1]   Wisdom, J.: *Problems of Mind and Matter,* Cambridge, 1934, p. 3.
[2]   Poincaré, H.: *La science et l'hypothèse,* Paris, 1923, p. 167.
[3]   Russell, B.: *Mysticism and Logic,* Pelican, edn., p. 46.
[4]   In fact many people may not like to enter a heaven peopled by angels whose substantial reality consists of nothing but the desires, feelings, hopes of all-knowing and exquisitely subtle minds. They should like also to relate to beings that can laugh and love and feel in the sense in which these terms indicate the presence of a soul, not only that of a mind. Moreover, they would

also object to finding themselves amongst eternal youths of beautiful physical forms enjoying an ideal nature deprived of soul. The soul is a wonderful fact. I cannot understand how it could have been ignored for so long by science and philosophy that have straightjacketed it into body and mind, unless it is that, as I have tried to show, philosophy and science have biased (weighted) the reality proper to conception and to perception to cover the totality of reality, where they are really part aspects and due only to an act of abstraction and an act of faith that is missing in the case of the *original* experience of the world as that qualitative whole of mind, body and soul, which we refer to as the experience of the common man.

5 Jung, C. G.: *The Practice of Psychotherapy*, Collected Works, Vol. XVI, London, 1954, pp. 46–7.

6 Jung, C. G.: *Two Essays on Analytical Psychology*, Collected Works, Vol. VII, London, 1953, p. 216.

7 Jung, C. G.: *Pyschology and Alchemy*, Collected Works, Vol. XII, London, 1953, p. 266, § 394.

PART II

TOWARDS A SCIENCE
OF THE SOUL

CHAPTER III

1: VERIFICATION

AS A SCIENCE progresses and its method is consolidated it begins to lose sight of both its humble empirical origins and its original principles. The foreground is occupied more and more by the contents of its immediate interests to the extent that all other possibilities of understanding come to be excluded from its point of view. Not only what it claims as true tends to become the only truth, but that of which it can predicate neither truth nor falsity loses reality value till it may disappear from its purview. Thus its methods of verification become the only admissible ones and its realities the only ones possible. This tendency is not only characteristic of science; it is also found in metaphysical systems, religious doctrines and art. For many people tonal music is the only music they can understand since its values are the only ones accessible to them — the depths and realities of other musical experiences being simply non-existent. Similarly many people committed to science fail to see that, in its essential qualities, namely, its disinterested quest for knowledge, its ethical neutrality and its open-mindedness, the spirit of science cannot be identified with any one specific scientific method and in particular that which has been developed to investigate the physical phenomena of the observable universe.

It follows that in psychology a failure to distinguish between the principle of science and its application means that those who seek to understand the soul scientifically necessarily reduce psychological truth to the verification criteria of physical science and its methods. Conversely, any psychologist who sees through this confusion and struggles in the dark groping for what is still to be discovered and affirmed will find his work criticised as unscientific where the term scientific carries the specific meaning of a physico-rational method of investigation. Such criticism, if correct, is misleading in the extreme, for it takes for granted the proposition that science and its principles of verification as we know them and have practised them for the past three hundred years are the only legitimate and valid possibilities of the spirit of science. Needless to say this proposition is neither logically necessary nor is there sufficient empirical evidence to support it when it is taken as an inductive conclusion from the observation of the evidence in question.

Now it is claimed by modern psychotherapy that its knowledge of the soul is the result of a scientific investigation as distinguished from such knowledge as was acquired in the past through religious practices, practical insight and personal experience. Therefore the claim of scientific psychology to formulate adequately psychological truths must be taken into serious account and examined in detail.

2: PSYCHOLOGY AND THE BODY

In the light of what we have said it is clear that the application of scientific methods for the investigation of physical phenomena will have most to show in those fields where their application has been the most adequate, namely, in so-called experimental psychology, which differentiates and classifies its material in terms of observable physical and chemical processes. The body and its means of adaptation to the world — its inner structure and its outer behaviour — can be observed and introspected by means of sense perceptions; in this respect the brain constitutes an integral part of the world of physical objects and consequently can be studied in much the same way as the control panel of a complicated computing machine. The correlation of cerebral processes with other physical processes in the body on the one hand and with behaviour on the other would thus in theory be sufficient to "explain" and "understand" human behaviour in general. Hence, psychological truth will be a function of reference to a specific theory organising the material and confirmed by observation of behaviour on the one hand and of neurological and cerebral processes on the other.

But in so far as psychology not only studies biological processes but also seeks to understand the mind and in so far as the mind is not either co-extensive with or equivalent to the brain, it follows that the validity of the conclusions of the experimental approach are dangerously threatened by the constant and unpredictable presence of the non-physical that is to say non-spatial, non-temporal realities of mind. If the body can influence and determine the mind it is also true that the mind can influence and determine the body. Therefore psychological truth established only on the basis of observation by means of sensible perception is liable to be overthrown by the intrusion of the non-physical factor.

In psychology, then, the validity of the empirical method in matters of human behaviour, governed as the latter is by mind, came up against a difficulty that was more than simply empirical. When science applied itself to the mind it found that it was limited by its methods and their reality values, for, if scienific truth depends on observation and confirmation by physical events, how can such a verification be possible in the case of mind where physical events are precisely and by definition ruled out?

Faced with this dilemma the science of psychology attempted to correlate mental events with physical ones and thus establish a bridge between the two worlds. All that was needed to safeguard the principles of scientific method was to postulate a verification for mental processes. This verification could only be validly accepted if it permitted observation or control of propositions referring to it. Propositions referring to mental processes are not verified by opening the skull and peering at the brain, nor can they be deduced or inferred with any degree of reliability from mere behaviour. They are verified by simply observing them with our mind. This observation of mind by mind is not to be confused with introspection which also includes the observation of physical processes. Rather it belongs quite clearly to what is commonly referred to as consciousness. Consciousness therefore is a prerequisite of a science of the soul, provided that that science has no other method and no other logic of verification than that imposed by the logic of observation as it applies to the physical world on the one hand and to the mental world on the other.

Now this position of a scientific psychology is in theory at least defensible. But when Janet discovered that large patterns of human behaviour were correlated with mental processes which however were inaccessible to direct observation by the subject, *i.e.* by his consciousness, but which nevertheless were such as to indicate overwhelmingly that they were present, the possibility of a scientific psychology on the lines above indicated was seriously endangered. And once Janet had shown that it was possible to *describe* mental processes and their physical correlates without reference to a perceiving, observing consciousness, the way was open for the genius of Freud to show us that such behaviour could also be *explained* not by reference to observable mental processes, that is to say, conscious ones, but to unobservable, that is to say, unconscious, mental events.

It cannot be too strongly emphasized that this possibility represents a major crisis for scientific method as it has been established and practised with respect to physical phenomena. For the requisite of any scientific proposition that is not *logically* necessary is that it should be verified by *experience;* it must be verified by observation through sense perception or by introspective mental observation. And this crisis of scientific method with regard to verification has rightly stimulated philosophers to clarify the issues.

In this respect verification of many of the propositions and theories of psycho-analysis depends logically and methodically on confirmation by observation and since such predictions are not confirmable in or by special arrangements as in empirical science but rather by *mental* observations it follows that only when what has been assumed is made conscious and is accepted can it be regarded as verifiable and hence validated or invalidated. Furthermore, in so far as the conscious verification of a previously unconscious mental event results in a modification of the correlative behaviour usually in the direction of a "cure" or disappearance of symptoms, it follows that the discovery of the mental unconscious event by the person in question and his confession of it is not sufficient as a *scientific* criterion of cure. Only when such a discovery is followed by the possibility of a public observation of adequate behaviour is the scientist entitled to talk of the truth of validity of the particular interpretation. This confusion in verification is most unfortunate. It means that the old dichotomy is once more reinstated, for it is again possible to judge, evaluate and verify mental processes by reference to behaviour criteria. Moreover it means that the science of the mind so magnificently developed by Freud is restricted to physical and medical concepts of behaviour and no more. The analysis of mind itself is left with the odium of being a half science, something that makes statements concerning the mind which cannot really be verified unless they can be correlated to something physical, to the body and its behaviour which all can see, feel, and touch. For, although verification in psycho-analysis looks like the problem of establishing motives and intentions in legal procedure, as a matter of fact it differs from such a process as say the unravelling of a crime. In the latter, for instance, the criminal can be caught and his confession verified by reference to other events in historical space and time, whereas in the former, confession and discovery of the unconscious processes cannot be verified by such references *unless* they cause, result, or somehow bring about a change in bodily behaviour which can be verified by observation.

In a science of the mind, therefore, verification criteria *must not refer us to a sense observable event* but rather to a mental event, which, though not observable is yet real because shared or shareable by all and objective to those sharing it in the sense that the proposition $2+2=4$ is objective to the man thinking it since it will also be true when his great-great-grandson will think it. In this sense of mind there certainly can be a science of mind and a science moreover that need not depend on the gymnastics of physical observation, but only on the confession and testimony of people, that in the long run and in the majority of cases provides just as valid a consensus as sense observation by the same people. Certain hypotheses as to whether this or that ultimate or general cause is true or not are not germane to the point under discussion. What is at issue is the fact that hypotheses can be formulated which refer us to non-physical factors as the origin of attitudes that, protean-like, retain their essence in the multitude of their expressions and transformations.

Freud's contributions to psychology therefore divide into two separate headings: firstly, the strictly clinical, therapeutic value as *psychopathology* whose rightful heir today is psychosomatics in the large sense of a science based on the working principle of a correlation of psycho-physical processes; secondly, the analysis of mind itself as a possibility on the same level as the analysis of physical phenomena and, hence, far beyond the limits of psychopathology and closer to a *general science of the mind*.

3: PSYCHOLOGY AND THE MIND

Freud's discovery of the possibility of investigating the mind scientifically meant that he was able to develop a genetic theory of mental processes and to show that what in the past had been explained in the language of ethics, religion, and philosophy, could in fact be explained on the basis of causal mental sequences. If we understand Freud's work in this light it becomes clear why he rejected philosophy, religion and ethics as obstacles to the progress of a science of the mind. Just as these disciplines were dispensed with when science discovered the possibilities of investigating nature, so too they can now be dispensed with in the case of the mind. Freud's methodology was therefore the first and most formidable opponent of these expressions of the human spirit as applied to the phenomena of mind. The mind as a whole is "natural" and therefore religious, ethical and philosophical values if important for social and political life are redundant to a strict science of the mind which regards them as no more than so many other expressions of its matter to be understood in terms of strict causal sequences. Thus the old descriptive psychology which saw mental processes in terms of conscious motivation such as intention, desire, wishes, and rationalizations, had to give way to the possibility of explanation of all these in terms not only of another series of unconscious motives but to the possibility of considering all these motives in turn as ultimately dependent on but a few generic ones.

But at this point the science of the mind had still to say where and of what nature were these ultimate motives, and it was here that psycho-analysis, sidestepped into philosophical materialism to consider this motivation to be ultimately bio-physical processes.

This thesis was criticised by Jung who, while adding to and enriching Freud's science of the mind, also deviated very much from it. In taking up Freud's discoveries Jung showed that certain mental processes could not be understood by reduction to events in the past nor could they be explained causally. By using the method of amplification in addition to that of free association invented by Freud, Jung was able to prove that mental processes were also teleological, that is to say, that chains of events could not be considered as entirely determined by the accidents of environment and constitution. The mind for Jung was goal-directed and therefore free in the sense that unpredictable paths could be taken in the achievement of a goal. Jung's concept of teleology differed from similar concepts in academic psychology whose explanations were long considered as teleological. Jung, like Freud, affirmed and proved the unconscious nature of these motives and processes. Thus while Freud introduced his conceptual interpretations of mind on a mechanistic model, Jung added the biological: the mind with its processes was analogous to a living organism with its processes and was accordingly to be understood by the same models as those appropriate to biology. Jung's concept of the unconscious in his investigation of mental phenomena acquired the purpose, plasticity, and spontaneous activity which we see in plant and animal life.

Thus if one aspect of science seeks to understand the multiplicity of causes in terms of one or two generic causal laws so too another aspect of science seeks to make clear the various goals by reference to one or two final factors that explain and co-ordinate all the others. In seeking for this factor, Jung, unlike Adler, rejected the hypothesis of a goal directed activity in terms of a purely social or biological aim. Clearly the aims and tendencies of the mind were not merely and only to subserve biological or social goals but pointed to some extra-mundane goal. Unlike any of his contemporaries Jung attempted to exploit the possibilities of a science of the mind to its utmost and avoid a philosophical interpretation of ultimate motives, or at least put it off as much as possible. To some this may seem, ironically enough, a strange way of presenting Jung's thought when most of his critics have brought out the mystical and so-called "unscientific" character of his psychology. But such criticism presupposes that science must adopt the philosophy of sense perception as the ultimate reality. If this is the case, mental processes must of course ultimately depend on biological ones, whether teleological or causal. But these assumptions are gratuitous, the more so when what we are here dealing with is specifically and by definition a science of the mind and not a science of psychosomatics where this presupposition has its proper place. Thus, all that Jung has asserted in his investigation of mental processes is that the ultimate causes and goals, the ultimate explanation of these must be considered as only in part biological and therefore as not ultimately physical or chemical. His concept of libido is illustrative of this point of view and will help us better to understand how, from a science of the mind Jung has slipped into and prepared the way for a science of the soul.

A determination to keep to the facts obliged Jung to formulate a concept of psychic energy which did not reduce it *a priori* to the instincts and which therefore oscillated between the possibilities of body and mind in terms of changes of potential. He was thus obliged to recognise an essential unity in this energy which unity however he had no way of establishing beyond the body-mind dichotomy. Thus his concept while useful was too general to admit causal or teleological explanations in terms of intra-mundane sequences since it did nothing to show us in what relation mind and body stood to one another and how and under what conditions energy passed from one to the other. Thus, as he himself confessed, his psychology of mental processes had to remain descriptive and his theory of integration and individuation was but the first tentative attempt at the formulation of a "motive" or generic "cause" or "purpose" behind the kaleidoscopic development of the material and which took into account the irreducible character of both spirit and instinct, mind and body.

Now the fact that his use of the concept of libido in this non-specific way produced results must therefore reflect a state of affairs not envisaged either by the mental or the biological sciences. For such a concept of psychic energy stands or falls if it corresponds to a reality that exists in its own right and through which this energy expresses itself. Such a reality we are now in a position to see does indeed exist and its omission from the modern world picture is a consequence of the dichotomy that has split the world into two and has thereby led us to lose sight of the soul, that *tertium quid* without which neither mind nor body have any meaning. Thus, while Jung never properly differentiated this reality from the mind and from the body, and while he often talks of psychological processes and means the contents of the mind and fantasy series, it is clear that his insistence on the reality of the soul could not be reduced to mental or physical processes without remainder.

In what follows therefore we shall concentrate upon showing that psychotherapy and its various branches, such as psycho-analysis and psycho-somatics, say nothing of the soul itself except as they manage to equate it with bodily or mental processes. While Jung himself has contributed largely to a science of the mind as was developed by Freud, he can also be said to have laid the foundations for a proper science of the soul. In consequence his work is the starting point of any investigation in this direction.

Thus, Jung's position in the history of psychology occupies a unique place. He was the first to use the terms "soul" and "psychological" to represent a reality independent of the philosophical prejudice of either the *esse in re* or the *esse in mente*. The *esse in anima* which is the basis of his credo, if not philosophically established, runs throughout his work and his thought as an empirical reality delimiting the field of psychological investigations.

4: PSYCHOLOGY AND THE SOUL

When modern psychology uses the terms psychic, psychological, as substitutes for mind or mental, talking of psychic or mental processes as equivalents, it is merely following the old body-mind dichotomy. This does a serious injustice to its field of inquiry. In the first place, motives such as wishes, intentions, hopes ideas, *etc.*, are mental processes but not psychological ones because the soul is not the motive or the mental process itself but refers to the experience of these. The explanation of a series of actions in terms of a power drive or a conscious intention working towards an end is not a psychological explanation because it says nothing of the value and the meaning of this, my action, and this, my motive, whether conscious or unconscious. It still makes sense to ask of any series of events (mental or body or both), whether they are also experienced by the subject in question — and this does not merely mean whether they were conscious or not or whether they were affectively charged or not. Neither the consciousness of a motive nor the affective value attached to it exhausts the meaning of psychological experience. Indeed, in the latter instance, one often finds the idea that soul means emotional, affective processes as opposed to the cold rational processes of the mind. It is clear however that the term "soul" has been used and is used without contradiction and in a perfectly legitimate sense to indicate trans-emotional states of existence or of experience such as the ideal of *apathia* in Stoic philosophy, or in the notion of a noble, dignified and reserved soul. Therefore neither the mind, nor the body, nor the affects, nor any combination of these can be considered as equal to the soul without remainder for the simple reason that mental, physical or affective processes are all so many possible sources of psychological experience as well as mediums through which that experience can be expressed.

In discussing the principles of a science of the soul therefore we must be constantly on the lookout for confusions of level which can lead us astray. Explanations in terms of biological drives, affective processes or reflex actions, whatever their legitimate value in their respective fields, cannot and must not be confused with psychological statements. Now, in such situations it is always advisable to ask for the verification criteria.

Verification involves two sorts of problems: firstly, what sort of facts are we to look for; and secondly, the actual nature of the evidence, its reliability and its generality. Freud's contribution to a science of mental processes was his discovery of motives such as wishes, desires, intentions, which could serve as causal factors to "explain" a series of mental events. His verification criteria accordingly passed over from those used by science in the case of physical or natural phenomena which could be sense perceived, to the order of mental "facts" which could not be sense perceived but could be verified nevertheless by introspection and private analysis. This was of course the only technique possible for psychology in general, and what Freud did was to construct concepts which brought all the various motives for action and for the particular course taken by series of mental events under one or two headings. It was this discovery of a generic causal nexus to which all other partial causes and motives could be significantly linked that psychoanalysis can be said to have established a valid scientific theory of the mind. However, the difficulty remains of establishing the nature of these generic causes as actual fact since they are clearly neither *a priori* nor deductively inferred from logically necessary propositions. And as these "causes" are not translatable into sense observable events but only into mental events, it follows that the evidence required can only be obtained as a result of a consensus. Unfortunately the degree of exactitude and the quantity of evidence at our disposal falls far below the requirements of science in so far as the value of personal testimony and the limited number of cases do not suffice to establish universal propositions as to the presence always and everywhere of such-and-such mental events. As Bernard Hart said in his excellent book, the difficulty does not consist only in verifying with any degree of exactitude the validity of the testimonies produced but furthermore belongs to the nature of the method itself with its high number of inferred rather than observed facts.[1] However the principle of a science of the mind has been established, whatever the practical difficulties in verifying the various conceptual constructions interpreting the "facts".

Thus, when a psychologist looks towards a mental fact or event for the verification of a statement, he is concerned with a science of the mind; and when, on the other hand he looks for verification towards a physical event or observable action whether in social life or in the sympathetic nervous system, he is concerned with the science of psychosomatics or psychopathology. In this connection Jung's work differs from psychopathology and Freud's psycho-analysis in that it uses a valuable model or conceptual construction for the interpretation of mental events such as dreams, fantasies, thought processes, *etc.* Furthermore, through the extension of that model into psychosomatics it offers another way of understanding and interpreting human behaviour wherever it is determined by or determines mental processes. But a science of the mind or that of the body or again psychosomatics is not on the same level as a science of the soul since the order of psychological facts is different from the orders of facts investigated by the former.

In establishing the principles of a science of the soul and its possibilities of a practical application as psychotherapy it will be necessary therefore to ask what sort of facts will be required to verify our concepts and what the nature of our conceptual system itself can be. It is clear that in the kaleidoscopic procession of psychological experiences there can only be observation and classification just as in the case of matters of sense-observable facts or of mental facts. And when it comes to interpretation it is clear that psychological facts cannot logically confirm or be verified by statements whose logical level belongs either to the order of behaviour or ideas. Here, Jung's statement that the truth of psychological realities is their effectiveness is not, strictly speaking, a verification criterion but only the affirmation of the reality of psychological experience. Again some philosophers and psychologists have looked towards a system of values. But a system of valuation, quite apart from its evident difficulty as to measurement, is so relative that it cannot serve the purposes of science which seeks to discover constant and universal factors. Furthermore, values themselves are not immediate psychological experiences but only the sources of expressions attached to these. The value of ugliness does not imply that the psychological experience of ugliness is necessarily itself ugly; on the contrary it may serve the purpose of creating a sort of purification and clarification. The problem of moral evil or sin is most instructive in this respect. The experience of sin does not necessarily add a negative value to that experience since it is always possible to assimilate and transform it. Through his soul man is free and not even the moral law can tie him down, otherwise the greatest teachings and the deepest experiences of the soul have been in vain.

It follows therefore that the meaning of psychological experience and psychological reality as defined in this work confronts us with an order of realities that is not be confused with those that belong to the body-mind dichotomy. It is because of this fundamental distinction that we have avoided discussing at any length or with any attempt at exactitude the important problems of verification and method in psycho-analysis and in analytical psychology. We have thought it enough to point out that *even depth psychology in its modern forms has not sufficiently grasped the distinction between a science of the mind and that of the soul.* The great exception to this is the work of C. G. Jung which, while it does not establish the principles of such a science, has acted and has developed on the presupposition that the soul is real and effective and that it is not the same as either mind, body, or both together. In what follows it is the spirit of method that will sustain us rather than this or that specific scientific method or truth criteria. By this means we hope to steer clear of inappropriate models and a misleading use of logic so as to try to discover the logic and the reality of our matter which will serve as the basis for an adequate logos of the soul and all the consequences that follow therefrom.

5: CONCLUSION

The field of inquiry which is proper to psychology is defined by the class of psychological experiences. This class is not the same as the class of material objects or of ideas. Therefore, the verification of any statement or theory concerning the nature, structure or working of the soul does not lie in the observation of physical processes, nor is it to be found in any mental process such as a wish, an intention, or a motive. Clearly it is to be found in psychological experiences. These are realities in their own right and therefore facts sufficient for our purpose springing directly from the reality and actuality of the soul. This consideration raises these problems: firstly, what is the nature of such observation; and, secondly, what is the logic of the theories interpreting the field of psychological experiences. In the latter case it is clear that any interpretation of psychological experiences which enables us to envisage a law must itself be a concept and therefore the subject of further psychological experience. In the former case, observation is not the same as simply objective perception or introspection or consciousness of ideas but must include that element of psychological experience proper which makes us differentiate between a report as registered by a photographic plate and a report as registered by a living soul. Hence both observation and explanation whereby psychological reality acquires order and meaning are very different in the science of psychology to what they are in either the science of material things or mental events. Moreover, by virtue of the peculiar position of the soul with respect to the mind and the body we cannot affirm only that the psychological field differs from the material or mental one but that it also includes or comprises these within its reality. In seeking to understand this reality we must therefore be prepared to abandon many of the recognised patterns of the conceptual networks which we throw over physical phenomena and mental fields in the processes of understanding and coming to terms with them. It is only then that psychological experience begins to acquire a meaning and a shape all its own by means of which we can understand and verify processes that are misunderstood and distorted by other systems. While the first part of this work was concerned with the delimination of this field what follows will be concerned with an effort to understand it and come to terms with it.

[1] Hart, B.: *The Psychology of Insanity,* 5th edn., Cambridge, 1957.

CHAPTER IV

1: MEANING IN PSYCHOLOGICAL EXPERIENCE

THE MANNER in which we have defined psychological experience implies an experiencing subject without which such experience is no different from mere registration or mentation. It is true, of course, that both mentation and perception imply also a thinking or perceiving subject but the distinction that holds between them and psychological experience is carried over to the problem of the subject as well. Thus, when the psychologist talks of the ego or the self he is faced with the problem of making it clear that the meaning of these terms is derived from the logic of the soul against whose background they move. He has to differentiate between the use of such terms in philosophy when we ask, for instance, "What is this willing, perceiving, thinking, acting part of man? This I, ego, soul, self, the subject of his mental states? Is it observable? Knowable? Is it a persistent stuff of some sort beyond its various modifications? Is it self knowing and if so, in what sense?" And what is its use in science, in those empirical contents where it is understood behaviouristically in terms of fields of forces, actions and reactions of a medium, however, whose unity is that of the physical and biological object and no more? And while he admits the validity of these two approaches in so far as they reflect the unity of body and mind as subjects of their states, the psychologist emphasises his own, namely, *the ego or self in psychology is the subject of the experiencing soul.* His primary concern is neither to introspect it nor describe it metaphysically as the philosopher tries to do, nor to observe it in so far as it affects and acts upon material events as the empirical scientist tries to do. He tries to seize it in terms of psychological experience where the meaning of experience is not that implied by the power to register perceptions or to formulate concepts but, including these, refers in addition to the possibility to experience as a soul. Thus the psychologist cannot substitute the subject of a mental state for the subject of the experience of the state. Soul and the ego are irreducible to other factors and refer to a living experiencing subject. From the depths of these experiences and their complexities firstly, through the experience of his own soul and, secondly, through that of others, grows what knowledge and what wisdom the psychologist possesses concerning the phenomena of psychological development.

Psychological reality, then, consists in the possibility of relating ideas, images, sensations, to an experiencing subject. Through this possibility of experiential relationship to a subject, there is born from psychological experience meaning and consciousness. For instance, it may well be that a thought can exist, but because it is not experienced psychologically and hence made meaningful through that experience, it remains theoretical and abstract. There are a great number of thoughts around that have yet to acquire psychological meaningfulness. Thus, *meaning in psychology refers to the experiencing soul and must be clearly differentiated from meaning as it relates to thought processes or as it is attached to sense perception.* The meaning of a landscape can be given in terms of an objective description of the various elements that constitute it and this can have meaning for a meteorologist, a biologist, a gardner, or an artist. But it is only when the landscape expresses a psychological experience that we can talk of its significance to the soul.

Of this production of meaning from psychological experience the psychologist can say nothing. It is a fact and it happens in much the same way as thought is produced by the brain. When, therefore, the psychologist talks of meaning and consciousness, he must be understood in reference to his background which is that of psychological experience. And if meaning in this sense presupposes the soul, conversely, to *understand* what the psychologist means by meaning and consciousness one must have understood what he means by psychological experience, and this is only in part a matter of definition and sense perception and essentially a matter of personal acquaintance in much the same way as acquaintance with colours implies vision permitting their perception.

The close connection that obtains between meaning and the experiencing soul is such, however, that it differs essentially from the logic of meaning as it obtains in matters of the mind. In the latter it is possible to consider meaning abstracted from the ego or self and forming part of an objective and absolute world outside and beyond the contingent subject. As a result of this abstraction science is able to formulate its concepts of law and its interpretative hypotheses ultimately confirmable by observation. Moreover, observation itself can also be abstracted to a considerable degree from the nuances of a particular observer to cover a kind of absolute observation, the ideal of which is the photographic plate. But the concept of universality and that of observation are established as far as possible independently and in spite of the limited and unreliable ego. It is clear, however, that this is not the case in psychology where the concept of an absolute or objective psychological experience independent of the subject experiencing it is impossible. Now in the case of a science of the mind, as depth psychology has recently developed it, the ego is conceived as an experiencing mind attached to the body, abstracted into an object suffering certain thoughts and undergoing the effects of organic transformations, but not essentially one with these thoughts or these physiological processes. In other words the ego can be considered on the model of an object like any other object in the world, and whether this object is conceived on the mechanical model as the panel of a complicated machine, or whether it is conceived biologic- ally as growing and developing like plants and living organisms do, it is not conceived as essentially one with its processes so that the ego *is* its thought or the ego *is* its body, but only in the dual form of here is the ego and there is the thought it has thought or the bodily movement it has made. These models adequate to science in the investigation of mind and body, therefore, break down in the case of psychological reality because the soul and the ego and the experience are all one indefinable and un- dissectible whole. Thus, whereas we can say that the ego and its body can be considered separately we cannot say that the psychological experience and the self experiencing it can also be so separated. There is no such thing as an objective psychological experience in the sense in which there is an objective perception of a material object. But there is such a thing as an objective psychological experience provided it also includes the subject, namely the self and the soul. Thus, there can never be such a thing as a photographic or mechanical registration of psychological experiences as there is in the case of sense perception, and there can be no such thing as a thinking machine or an electronic brain as there can conceivably be in the case of mental operations. This unique position of the soul and the self has defied modern science and modern philosophy simply because these are split essentially into the body-mind dichotomy so that the very structure of their language and the only models at their disposal necessarily divide their field of enquiry into two and hence, in the case of psychological experience, inevitably separate the subject from the experience from its significance.

These considerations lead us therefore to reformulate the role which interpretative theory or the meaning of psychological experience can play in our investigations of the soul on the one hand, and the nature of observation on the other hand. The universality of meaning essential to scientific hypothesis, and the objectivity of observation essential to proof and confirmation, presuppose a very different set of factors to those obtaining in body-mind fields. It is to the discussion of these two aspects of psychological investigation that we must now turn.

Universality of meaning in the field of psychological experience is not to be confused with any generality which may result from the observa- tion of a great number of individual cases. That is to say we are dealing with the difference between law and the instances that confirm it. But unlike the fields of body or mind, law in psychological experience cannot be separated from an experiencing subject and hence any objectivity and universality of meaning attached to the soul must be closely related to such a creative and experiencing subject. This raises a problem the importance of which cannot be underestimated since there is nothing in the ego or in individual experience which alone justifies the existence of universal meanings and transpersonal psychological principles. At best we have an accumulation of individual experiences, which clearly can never pass into the logical plane of universality. Thus, we are confronted from the very outset both by logical and empirical limits imposed by the subject or ego which do not exist in classical science. We must therefore examine more closely the ideas of transpersonality in its connection to universal principles.

When we qualify psychological experience as the possibility of relationship to an ego we mean that this possibility would, in theory at least, be within the range of experience of the ego were it to cross the field in question. The same conditions, of course, hold in the worlds of material objects and ideas. In all these instances the world is much larger than it presents itself to a perceiving, conceiving subject at any one moment. Moreover, there are definite limits to the range of qualitative experience of the world as well. Thus the range of perception and the capacity of conception are closed at both ends although under exceptional circumstances they may be considerably extended. The psychological self is no exception to this state of affairs and is limited both qualitatively and quantitatively. One sense of transpersonality is expressed by Pascal when he says: "Tous les hommes ensemble, y font un continuel progrès, à mesure que l'humanité vieillit, parce que la même chose arrive dans les successions des hommes que dans les âges différents d'un particulier. De sorte que toute la suite des hommes, pendant le cours de plusieurs siècles, doit être considérée comme un même homme qui subsiste toujours et qui apprend continuellement." [1] The psychological self can be here considered to be in a state of continual evolution so that transpersonality would then mean this superordinate self which belongs to humanity and which has been formed during the years of experience through which mankind has passed in its history. Such an interpretation, however, is but one of the possibilities of transpersonality, because though we can envisage the constant extension and enrichment of experience and the range of the self this remains qualitatively limited. In this latter sense the development of personality will not refer to the indefinite extension of the world of psychological experience, of sense perception and of thought, but rather to the harmonious development of its totality in the sense of a pre-established pattern. With the exclusion of the spirit from the world and its banishment to the transcendental it was thought that such an ideal of perfection and completion within the world could be attained provided man recognised its limits. Thus philosophy cut itself off from speculative and transcendental metaphysics and science, from extra-sensory or extra-corporeal possibilities. Psychology following the modern spirit of humanism is easily tempted to do likewise. Consequently we should not be surprised to discover that most modern psychological theories limit the range and power of the soul to its relationship with the human subject or ego consciousness and refuse to see further except in the direction of a quantitative extension such as extra-sensory ranges of perception or the possibilities of extraordinary experiences. As regards personality they are content with a concept of the soul as individual and collective, that is to say, related to an individual, a social group, race and genus. An analogous concept of psychic energy moreover provides a more or less adequate possibility of understanding the pathology and goals of personality within their individual and social framework.

Entirely different from these two interpretations of transpersonality is the situation when we envisage the possibility of the existence of meanings that transcend the powers of the ego or any collectivity of egos to grasp and which nevertheless are in the world and claim recognition. Such, for instance, are the basic facts of life and death, rebirth, immortality, as bearers of meanings that transcend the ability of individual or group egos to realise. In such cases it is not what they may come to mean to the ego but the fact that they pose a problem at all that points to the mystery and the transpersonal significance.

Confronted with the presence of this challenge of transpersonal and universal meanings the psychologist cannot affirm their existence in terms of a law or a theory as in physics or in metaphysics unless he also and by definition presupposes a self to which they can be related. This was the step of major consequence taken by Jung when he formulated his hypothesis of a superordinate personality though there is a great deal of ambiguity as to whether this "self" represents a sort of abstracted condensation of individual experiences and racial memories, or whether it is strictly speaking a universal and ontological reality qualitatively different from the ego. In the former case the hypothesis of a self differs little from Pascal's notion of the same man developing through the succession of generations. In the latter case, however, the universality of meaning qualifying psychological reality as it relates to the transpersonal self will correspond to an objective and ontological possibility the equivalent of which in physics and in mind is the concept of law or principle. The difference here between psychology and mathematics and physics is that principles and laws in the latter case can be discovered independently of the contingent subject whereas law in psychology presupposes by definition a subject, and since the contingent ego cannot be the subject of universal principles the possibility of such principles must be connected with an equivalently universal subject.

We cannot at present go into all the grounds which justify this point of view or the meaningfulness of experiences that later confirm it. But when a man lives his life in terms of a meaningfulness of psychological experiences that recognises nothing beyond his human ego or the social organisation of a group or race to which he belongs then, however harmonious and humanistic this man's horizon may be, nevertheless, the ultimate meaningfulness of his life, his individual powers to create and sustain the spirit of a creative culture, will be seriously restricted. The establishment of meaning over and above the individual ego is imposed on us by the facts and by the logic of psychological experience and *presupposes a transpersonal subject* in addition to objective law *thus differing fundamentally from both physics and mathematics,* for whom the existence of such a subject, though possible in speculation as, for instance, in the idea of a mathematician god, is not essential to the discovery and establishment of universal relationships.

The existence of meaning whether individual or transpersonal requires, however, confirmation in terms of reality. In science such confirmation has come through the reality of the phenomenal universe perceived through the senses. In depth psychology, as it extends to the mind, such verification refers us to mental facts which, though not sense observable, are mind observable, that is to say, can be discovered as present in the mind in the form of wishes, intentions, desires, hopes, whether conscious or unconscious. Having rejected depth psychology in its present form as adequate to a science of the mind but not taken as a science of the soul, it is clear that whatever meanings attach to psychological experience must be confirmed and verified on the same logical level, namely, psychological experience itself. This raises the problem of how we are to formulate or observe this experience and whether what we understand by "observation" does not differ in important respects from what it implies for sense perception and for mentation.

2: OBSERVATION

The formulation of hypotheses in psychology requires confirmation neither by observation of physical events nor by mental processes but by the observation of psychological experiences. Verification in psychology is on the same level as the facts from which the original theories are drawn and to which they apply. But the observation of psychological experience poses problems of a specific nature not found in either the physical or mental sciences. We therefore have to consider firstly the question, how does one observe psychological experiences at all, and secondly, whether such observations satisfy the conditions for the verification of scientific hypotheses.

In the first case it is clear that observation of the soul on the same lines as we observe the twitching of a stimulated muscle or the behaviour of rats in a maze or the customs of the Zulus is not at all possible because in this sense of observation all that we actually observe are physical events and not psychological experiences. The only model which will do for us is that which applies to the meaning we attach to the observation of a tragedy, a drama, or ritual. The observation of a tragedy has a logic of its own comparable neither to the reports of the camera nor to the introspection of inner processes whether they may be a description of how I feel, what I see, or what emotions I experience. It involves a participation with what is observed so that the spectator cannot abstract himself from the objective facts he is observing while these facts are not exhausted by a mere description of what he sees, feels or hears.

For instance, a complete report of the sequence of events in Shakespeare's *Macbeth* is not the same as to say that I have seen or observed the play *Macbeth*. Moreover, a description of my feelings and emotions during the play is again not what we mean when we say we saw the play *Macbeth*. Such observations differ from the report of an eclipse or the report of a trial to establish motives, causes and responsibilites. In the latter cases there is a sense of objectivity which does not obtain in the former. In fact the only way I can convey my observation of the play to someone who has not seen it is to go over the story as carefully as possible and hope that he will grasp its meaning where the meaning, however, does not reside in an analysis of the story or a historical description of events. The meaning is in the drama and the drama releases its meaning only when it is experienced. This interpretation of observation may seem to be stretching the point but "observation" like "experience" has suffered a consistent distortion in favour of sense perception and at the expense of experience where experience implies participation and perception through the soul. Every psychologist knows that a report of what went on in a psychotherapeutic session gives no idea of what actually took place and looks more like a cross examination than the living, subtle, and indefinable quality of the experience as lived through both by the patient and the analyst. Thus, to organise the material from a report of such sessions with a view to explanation and solution would be like proceeding to analyse *Macbeth* on the lines of a detective story. Now, no one denies, of course, that what goes on in a psychotherapeutic session between two individuals involves much more than a search for motives and for forgotten memories, just as, of course, no one denies that the experience of the tragedy of *Macbeth* is different from the problems of motive and responsibility in a crime. But what interests the psychologist is not merely the affirmation that these situations are qualitatively different from legal investigations or physical explorations but that they should be possible of circumscription and delimitation so that they can serve as a field of scientific investigation. Up to the present the psychologist has had to translate such experiences into behaviour patterns on the one hand and mentative processes on the other, because these were the only fields where science provided him with adequate models to work upon. Such a procedure has been rightly criticised by poet, philosopher, and priest as killing the thing one seeks to study. In point of fact it is less a killing of the soul than a distortion of its field of reality.

Once, therefore, we accept the homogeneity and qualitative unity of psychological experience we must resist the temptation to interpret the observation of this field in terms of sense perception and regard it much more on the model of observation in the sense discussed above. *Psychological experience, like dramatic experience, is observable only if the observer has participated in the event, that is to say, has registered the event as experientially meaningful to him.* The observation of psychological experience covers more than an account of behaviour or thought processes to which affect has been attached and implies in addition an indefinable yet universally known experience that takes place every time we participate in and express ourselves through the soul. We cannot therefore be accused of inventing a new unit of experience but only of attempting to differentiate for purposes of understanding an experience as old if not older than humanity and which has expressed itself through ritual, drama, and art.

Now two of the prerequisites of science are abstraction and objectivity, and, given the nature of psychological experience, it may well be asked how such conditions can be obtained when, unlike either the fields of matter or that of thought, the "objects" to be observed cannot be by definition separated from the observing and experiencing ego. Under these circumstances the scientist feels that he will betray the ethics of science if he were to consider his matter in the manner of art and drama, that is to say, indissolubly linked with the ego; moreover, were he to accept the unique quality of psychological experience which he is asked to observe not as a camera reports a parade but as a participator of a drama, he may well wonder how the dividing between the observer and that which he observes can be established.

The difficulties raised by this question have been to a certain extent already answered by depth psychology which has revealed to us that psychological experience does indeed possess an objectivity and integrity of its own comparable to that of works of art, ritual, and drama, thanks to which we can appreciate genuine productions from spurious ones, good art from bad art, effective ritual from false and illusory pseudo-ritual.

In psychotherapy this objectivity takes the form of a departure from the old technique of suggestion and persuasion whereby the doctor's ego tries to modify and act directly upon his patient's psychic system towards a recognition of the autonomy and self-habilitating power of the psyche. Respect for the other has ceased to be an ethical theorem for the psychotherapist but a methodological and practical necessity. And such respect could hardly have led the way to the discovery of the self-habilitating powers of the soul if there were not already a possibility of differentiating, in practice at least, between the observer's psychological experience and observations and those belonging to the subject.

These two characteristics of psychological experience, its subject-object unity and its dramatic quality, place the psychologist in a delicate position with respect to criteria of cure. The change from maladjustment of social and personal values towards adaptation and adjustment may well be a condition of cure in psycho-physics, but it cannot serve as a criterion in psychology because *neither the mental condition nor bodily behaviour are of themselves sufficient to confirm a psychological statement concerning the soul.* In this sense a well-adapted individual whose brain functions normally and whose body shows no symptomatic behaviour may need no psychotherapy but may nevertheless be leading a very poor life of the soul. On the other hand certain behaviour disturbances and certain mental eccentricities may well indicate a deep psychological experience which cannot be understood in terms either of social adaptation or of physical health but only in those of the phenomenology and logic of the soul.

The phenomenology of the soul, however, covers processes of a fluidity and plasticity that are not possible of fixation as in the case of the science of physical events or mental forces. The same psychological experience may express itself in a hundred different ways and in fundamentally different mediums: for instance, through music, pictorial art; through a philosophical thought or a bodily gesture. The idea, therefore, that we can fix such meanings by formulation in a scientific language is a prejudice of an overintellectualised culture and a misunderstanding of the limits of certain specific scientific methods. For it is clear that whatever the language into which we translate the experience, that translation is not the same as the experience that has already been expressed in a perfectly communicable medium. A criticism of a moving poem reveals nuances and may itself be an enrichment of our experience of the poem but cannot be considered as a substitute for that experience in the sense in which "x" can function in a mathematical formula for a material object. If this is so, then there is no common measure in psychology whereby we can formulate in one language the same experience expressible through a poem or a gesture (a love sentiment). *The facts of psychology, therefore, have no possibility of formulation in a common reference language and can only be conveyed by repetition of the event.* This is of course consonant with the character of drama and art in general; and our assimilation of psychological experience to these phenomena is therefore all the more justified. It explains, moreover, why so many people are fascinated by case histories in psychological books and also why there can be no science (as it stands at present) of mythology, of folklore or of religion and drama, in so far as these affect the soul, because the language in which this experience is expressed is not only the best possible formulation of that unique experience but is un-translatable into any other language without an essential loss of meaning and distortion of reality content. At most, we can say that translation augments the experience by adding a new element to it but cannot be considered as expressive of the original. On the contrary, to believe that the translation is an adequate rendering of the experience in the sense that a report of the sequences and events in a tragedy is considered as an adequate rendering of the tragedy in question leads to a multiplication of error since the translation itself becomes in its turn a source of psycho-logical experience. To translate the soul into behaviour patterns or mentative processes means that such translations in turn condition and determine further psychological experiences that will rapidly lead to an almost complete loss of soul for the individual or culture that has placed its faith in such methods.

Thus the problem of observation in psychology presents itself as a question of phenomenological approach where, however, the phenomena observed can only be reported, formulated, and communicated by repetition of the original experience. Both interpretation and formulation of the experiences observed are therefore modified accordingly and point the way to a new understanding of the meaning of the processes of the soul in general and psychotherapy in particular.

3: INTERPRETATION AND FORMULATION

As we have seen, psychological experience is composed of a qualitative whole from which the content experienced cannot be separated from the experiencing subject without loss of meaning. Now, if in one sense we can refer to the experiencing subject as a self ego, in another sense such a term is inappropriate when we desire to refer to the totality of the experience as a living, self-sufficing and homogeneous whole. In this connection we use such terms as "personality", "character", and "individuality". However, while modern psychology may be clear as to what it means when it refers to individuality and character the problem of personality and its closely allied concept of genius still baffles and challenges the scientific psychologist. The reason is not far to seek. Whereas in both individuality and character we are dealing with certain specific psycho-physical concepts, personality defies reduction to description in terms of mental attitudes and behaviour patterns. The problem of personality only makes sense if we place it in its rightful context, namely, the meaningful wholeness of the soul. An understanding of the problems of personality therefore will depend on the possibility of formulating and interpreting psychological experiences, and conversely the possibilities of formulating and interpreting psychological experience are themselves products of the action of personality.

This paradoxical and unorthodox position with respect to the possibilities of scientific formulation of psychological realities appears to have blocked any progress science could have made in matters of the soul since science restricted its method of analysis and interpretation of psychological experience and its meaningfulness to the logic of sensible perceptions (emotions, feelings, physical events) on the one hand and to the logic of mentative processes (conceptual formulation of wishes, motives, intentions, etc.) on the other. Thus, while science is able to analyse character and individuality in terms of their physical and mental experience constituents it is unable to explain thereby the illusive but essential and indefinable quality of personality which belongs to every person who is moved by a soul as well as by a body or mind.

In trying to analyse and understand psychological experience, therefore, we realise that we are dealing with qualitative units of the personality that cannot be broken up into their constituent parts without remainder because the whole in such cases is over and above its parts or any combination of these. Personality or its various manifestations cannot therefore be described or interpreted in the usual manner because such description would subject the contents described to the logic of the language and, unless such language was that of the soul, would result in a distortion of the original experience. Personality and hence the meaningfulness of psychological experience is prior to the language in terms of which it is to be described. In other words personality, like the logic of the soul, is a reality unto itself. But it is not as psychological experience that it is understood or lived but rather as the meaning of that experience released by it and contained within it.

The difficulty of expressing personality imposed on modern consciousness by the dichotomy of the language of science and philosophy has been responsible for talk of a third dimension in life, of a super-rational faculty, and has created pseudo esoteric language by means of which this experience is conveyed. Of course, it is very easy for the philosopher and scientist to destroy what semblance of meaning such languages may contain, but on the other hand, their failure to grasp the significance of the facts behind the drive often leads them to a loss of soul that makes both philosophy and science today so impotent with respect to the values of personality. Conversely, others tend to travel the opposite extreme and equate the meaningfulness of the soul with an ideology of the body or a mysticism of the inner life in terms of dreams, fantasies and visions. Thus, the body or the psychoid world are overvalued and, consequently, present themselves as philosophies of life in terms of such concepts, for instance, as life force, or in the mysticism of spiritualistic movements. The origin of whatever meaning and fascination belongs to these formulations resides, however, not in the living body or the dream but principally in the meaningfulness of psychological experience which a distorted language and an inadequate world outlook are incapable of integrating.

Psychological interpretations, therefore, and the language in which they are formulated are a function of the meaning of psychological experience which is centred in the existence of personality, Psychology, therefore, as a science must necessarily place its logic before its empiricism from which the latter acquires direction and significance. The consequence of this point of view is the rectification of personality which, subject as it was either to descriptions in terms of bodily behaviour or mental qualities, can now be regarded as primary to them so that they themselves can be understood by reference to it. It follows that personality of which the intelligible centre is psychological experience becomes a principle and a symbol which is but partly seized by mind or described in terms of body and which, on the contrary, has its own meaning so that both body and mind acquire significance as a result of being integrated into and seen through personality.

In psychology, therefore, both interpretation and formulation are functions of that indivisible and qualitative whole which we call personality and which carries its own meaning released through psychological experience and its processes. In such cases psychological statements must be understood as references to the meaning of psychological experience for a given personality and cannot be translated into or reduced to the language of perception or mentation but are either understood in the same way as tragedy and drama and ritual are understood or not at all.

Scientific explanation, as is well known, proceeds by formulating interpretative concepts, hypotheses or laws which it then seeks to verify by reference to matters-of-fact. It would follow, therefore, that a science of the soul should proceed along the same line, namely, the formulation of interpretative theories and their confirmation by reference to the realities of psychological experience. However it is clear that interpretative concepts are significant in terms of the thinking rational mind and not in terms of the meaningfulness of personality. (Therefore, in psychology it can be said that there can be no verification of hypotheses because the language in which they are formulated is not of the personality but only of the mind.) Thus, although explanation in terms of rational concepts in psychology may well form part of our understanding of psychological experience, it should not be confused with our point of reference which remains in respect to the logic of our field the meaning of personality as it emerges from psychological experience. How, it may be asked in that case, is this meaning expressed at all? The answer to this question takes us to the core of the matter inasmuch as it forces upon us the realisation that the medium of expression of the meanings of the soul is the symbol. The symbol therefore functions in psychology in the same way as the concept functions in a science of the body and of the mind. Confirmation of the truth and validity of the symbol come not by reference to a matter-of-fact or an idea but by reference to what we may call the realisation of the ontological status of the reality expressed by the symbol. Just as a thought needs to be related to a matter-of-fact, so too the symbol needs to be related to an ontological reality and this reality, as we have seen, is no other but that of the soul. The criticism that there is no criterion to the indefinite possibilities of symbolic interpretations and formulations is as applicable to our field as the criticism of any of the innumerable theories as to natural phenomena which can be formulated in the case of science. In the latter case the touchstone of reality and truth is the degree to which the theory can be related to matters-of-fact and through such a relationship explain and predict them. Similarly, in the former case symbolic interpretations are not valid unless they are related to psychological experience and confirmed by such experience which, moreover, as we have seen, depends ultimately on a *consensus gentium* and evidence by testimony that is as valid as that of sense perception or of mentation. By defining and delimiting the field of psychological experience psychology and psychotherapy differ from the classical symbolic-mythological interpretations of the world as well as from the modern intuitive cultural psychologies in that they have differentiated an empirical basis for their interpretations which, therefore, can be referred to a reality that is lived and experienceable in the here and now, and hence are possible of correction and verification.

It may be urged that the value of science is its principle of converging simplicity and that such a principle has yet to be established in psychology. However, a moment's reflection will show us that the various possibilities of significant experiences that ramify from an individual psyche are related to one another by means of a centre the essence of which is, on the one hand, the self or ego and on the other, the superordinate personality which we have anticipated as a universal and transpersonal principle. In this sense, personality will have a double meaning: firstly, in so far as it refers to the simplicity and unity of converging meanings of a personal and temporal psychological totality; and secondly, in so far as it refers to the Oneness and Totality of a transmundane psychological reality.

Interpretation and formulation, therefore, in psychological experience do not necessarily rule out the possibilities of investigation demanded by the spirit of science. What they do rule out is the specific method adequate to the investigation of physical and mental realities. On the other hand, provided we include the spirit of science in the formulation of a symbolic language checked by the realities of psychological experience we have every reason to believe in the creative possibilities of a science of the soul which can also become a therapy of the soul in the fullest meaning of the term. Indeed, the unity and relatedness of psychological experience, its intimate connection to the body and to the mind, and its release of meaning through this experience that is both life and thought encourage us to hope that the mystery of the soul contains within itself the solution to the cosmos that can be and indeed demands to be realised by man, firstly, through his mundane personality and, secondly, but originally and finally, through his transmundane personality which is both universal law and Self consciousness.

The close connection that obtains in psychology between the ego and its experiences is such that method in psychology cannot be separated from the personality to which it is applied. Moreover, such a connection implies that the application of the method and the destiny of the soul to which it is applied are also very closely connected; hence, psychological development and particularly the possibility of cure and the application of the method ride tandem with one another. In psychology more than anywhere else we must always be aware that we can only see and obtain from our matter what we put into it in the form of preconceptions and methodological systems. The object of psychology, therefore, while it can be described in general as the object of any science, namely, knowledge, and in particular, knowledge of the soul, is indissolubly linked with the fact that such knowledge is not an abstract of causal series as in the material universe but is valid, that is to say, confirmable only through personality or psychological experience and its meanings to a self. Thus, knowledge in psychology is also life and life means, specifically, the development of personality. Where no such development takes place there is no validity to the knowledge or the method by means of which it was acquired since the only criteria of verification are those provided by psychological experience and hence personality. The adequateness of the method lies, therefore, not only in the theories and their confirmation but in the growth of personality that takes place as a result of the application of the method. In fact, the latter possibility is easier to observe and verify than the former since, as we have seen, psychological experiences are essentially fluid and multiform whereas the evidence of personality, though not measurable quantitatively, is at least experienceable by oneself as well as by others whose reports and evidence we have as much reason to believe as we do those of the artist, the explorer, and the scientist. Psychological method, therefore, differs from psychosomatics. Both seek for verification and confirmation of the validity of their method in the possibilities of cure: the latter possesses certain specific criteria of cure that are measured in terms of bodily health (perceivable and checkable) on the one hand, and ego adaptation to the demands of society and the individual personality on the other hand; equally observable, the former has no such criteria inasmuch as psychological experience and the maturation of personality are not one with such adaptations but point to factors and meanings beyond them. In this sense the notion of cure of the personality or its development is not observable in terms of psycho-physical concepts but is established by personal testimony and evidence provided by others who have not so much observed but experienced the personality in question. Such evidence, as we have seen, is not at all less real or dependable than that provided by physical observation or mental calculations; it refers us to the common world of the reality of the soul common to all and experienceable by all, in and through which we live as we live through and participate in a body and a mind and as a result of which our perceptions and conceptions can be communicated and shared by all.

4: CONCLUSION

The peculiar and intimate connection that obtains between psychological experience and its significance is analogous, though not reducible, to the relation that obtains between a proposition and the sentence expressing it. But unlike the relation between reason and physical events the interpretation, observation and formulation of psychological experience do not depend on an impersonal language and objective observation; but, on the contrary, both that which is observed and the language in which it is formulated are essentially conditioned by the experiencing subject as they are also themselves objects of experience to that subject. Thus the psychologist finds himself combining the functions of an empirical scientist with those of a theoretician; he is grammarian and logician, logician and philosopher, and his field of inquiry which includes, firstly, the observation and formulation of psychological experience and, secondly, the interpretation of that experience in terms of its psychological significance, is essentially related to an experiencing subject constituting what we refer to as personality. Thus personality and its nucleus the self are the logical limits of psychology. *Furthermore the significance of personality acquires thereby the significance which in science and philosophy attaches to universal law.* For just as individual events serve to show forth the law which they obey, so too individuals show forth the universal principle of personality. Thus individual personalities are embodiments of a personality principle which is transindividual and universal.

Now, whereas it can be said that scientific reason seeks to discover the universal laws that obtain between contingent events, psychological investigations dominated as they are by the presence of personality can be said not only to discover the principles of personality that obtain in matters of psychological experience but by reason of this discovery to actually effect a change in the individual personality both of the observer and of the observed. Thus the discovery of law in psycholgy is also a realisation of that law in its relation to a personality whose significance affects and conditions further psychological experiences. Hence, unlike the exact or the empirical sciences, the discovery of the significance of psychological experience and the realisation of personality are essentially interconnected. *Method in psychology therefore* acquires an importance that far exceeds that which it possesses in the other disciplines. *For it is both a means of becoming, as well as a means of discovery.* There is no possibility of detaching method from ethical, religious and philosophical considerations as there is in the sciences. Thus psychological method does not only imply a means to the discovery of universal relations but includes also such parascientific considerations as those which help us to use scientific knowledge for ethical, religious, and philosophical ends inasmuch as these are important components of personality. As we have seen, a clear understanding of the presuppositions of the method is imperative if we are to arrive at a just notion of the laws underlying psychological processes because these processes are not only objective to the method but can be said to be determined, conditioned and changed by the very process of applying the method at all. Such is not the case in classical science where physical nature can be investigated by methods which do not affect their authenticity and objectivity. This independence of method from its field of application means that the scientist can abstract his practice from considerations as to what he is to do with and how he is to use whatever knowledge he hopes to acquire through his pursuits. In psychology, on the other hand, the question of how we are to use our knowledge of the soul and what the effects of investigation upon both the object and the subject will be are questions of primary importance and have to be faced at the moment when the psychologist decides to investigate the soul at all. Justifications for his procedure and an answer to the question why he pursues science at all, must be forthcoming and are demanded of him and commit him to an act of faith with respect to the consequences of his research which in the case of the scientist can be indefinitely postponed or easily passed over as beyond the range of pure scientific enquiry. *Verification in psychology therefore demands that every step forward, every hypothesis that is checked and confirmed, should also satisfy the values of the soul and hence be itself a means towards their realisation.* Thus what a psychologist comes to know about the soul qualifies him in a way that scientific knowledge can never qualify the scientist. For the scientist it is always possible indeed, it is imperative that he should divorce his personality from what he knows and from the matter to which this knowledge applies: the application of his method is independent of its effects on him and his investigations are carried on in spite of rather than through his personality. Not so the psychologist who, at the same time as he studies his world, is creating it as well as creating himself. Such a creation means that the responsibility of its consequences attaches itself directly to its creator, whereas the responsibility for the creations of science disappears behind the anonymity of abstract thought and impersonal law passing the problem of the use of such knowledge, whether for good or for bad, on to others who are supposed to know somehow to deal with it adequately. Nevertheless as science advances it tends to whittle down the differences that separate it from the normative and philosophical disciplines without however adequately providing for suitable justification of its ways or its possibilities of application. The result is that the further we advance in scientific knowledge the more we are threatened by the irrational and the unknown in man's nature, and the more we seem to be exposed to the evil that lies within us and for which science does not prepare us. If psychology, therefore, forgetting its original premises, sacrifices to the exigencies of a specific scientific point of view, it is highly probable, as it has been clearly evidenced in recent times, that the knowledge so acquired will not be in relation to the problems of realisation of personality and the goals of psychological development as well as the problems of justification which essentially condition such development. The more we know the further away we will move from the realisation and significance of personality and the reality of the soul on which it is based. Thus the present circumstances of world affairs and the logic of the soul itself alike impose upon us a clarification of the presuppositions of psychological methodologies and teach us reserve before all attempts to investigate human behaviour and human intelligence by principles that do not take into account the fact that these have a meaning for psychology only if they are seen against the background of psychological experience and realised in terms of the significance of personality. The disorientation in the world and the loss of soul which is its most serious consequence result from the original dichotomy that has split reality into body and mind at the expense of the soul. Hence any attempt that seeks to unify knowledge and life, science and spirit on the basis of an original and creative but none the less actual and empirical reality, that is to say, on the basis of both a practical possibility of research as well as a theoretical possibility of understanding, should be worth our effort. Seen in this light psychological method is not merely a technique but is also a way, and a way moreover that goes far beyond the limits of a scientific therapy whose goals are defined from the outside, so to speak. The goals of a logos of the soul are unknown and await discovery because the soul, if it is limited by the body and its exigencies and if it is amenable to mind, nevertheless plumbs depths and points to possibilities beyond the immediate goals of this mundane and brief existence. This means that the psychologist has to plunge inside his matter and become one with it, so to speak, so that the man and the method are one.

Thus the problems of observation, interpretation and formulation in psychology converge towards one point, namely, the theory and application of method. And, as we have seen, the use of any method in this field presupposes an act of faith that sees in method also the principles and ways of the development of personality in both its individual and transpersonal realities. Thus, while the problem of method which will occupy the next chapter may be conveniently divided into a theoretical and a practical aspect, we will have to be aware that these condition one another in a way that is not the case in science, so that the justification and the achievement, the goal of the process and the purpose of the investigator, are inseparable from one another. Indeed, there can be no truth in psychology that is not also a realisation, and hence the presence of the knowledge myth, while tolerated in the natural and the exact sciences, cannot be so in psychology where any goal which remains unrealised or unrealisable directly affects the investigator and qualifies his methods. And while science can pass on to other disciplines, ethical and epistemological considerations, the science of the soul cannot do this without serious injustice to the principles of its subject matter inasmuch as these are valid subjects of psychological experience and qualify the aspirations and spirit of personality. The Ideal and reality, object and subject in psychology, meet in the common field of the soul whose significance is a mystery the solution of which resides in personality and its vivifying and spiritualising centre, the self. Then, while the principles of method in psychology determine and delimit the logical boundaries of the soul, the application of the method cannot be separated from the problems of the realisation of personality and the goals which have moved and move man not only to knowledge but to the affirmation of such knowledge as a being and an ultimate goal and hence a redemption of that which is known through the act of knowledge as it emerges from the soul of the knower and addresses itself to him and through him to others.

[1] Pascal, B.: *Pensées,* V.

ADDENDA

EXCERPTS FROM NOTEBOOKS
AND LETTERS

Explanation does not produce meaning. Meaning is prior to explanation. An explanation is an answer to a question and particularly to the question "why?" But this "why?" must make sense in the first place. The simple fact that "why?" can be asked at all is the basis for talking of the presence of meaning in the world.

*

The interpretation of unconscious material must take place in accordance with all we know and hence in accordance with metaphysical theories as well.

In psychological experience it is not the causal factor that is prominent but the integrative one. It is a matter of consciousness of things as they are, not of their causes.

*

The trouble with cultural psychologies is that they are unable to establish an empiricism of psychological experience, only one of motives and philosophical attitudes. For it is clear that psychology should not be oriented to the understanding of motives but to the understanding of psychological *experience*. This is the matter, the reality, on which and from which any understanding must come.

*

A science of the soul, to be true to psychological experience and its logos, has to meet conditions that do not obtain in matters of the body or of the mind.

Firstly, it interprets and formulates psychological facts through the experiencing ego so that the affirmation of particular or general propositions implies a particular or general subject to which the meanings of these propositions must be attached. Thus both the ego and the trans-individual personality are not constructed out of or after the observation of certain facts but form part and parcel of those facts themselves and without which these would no longer be psychologically significant.

Secondly, the peculiar nature of psychological experience and its meaning directly clashes with certain conditions which are considered as essential to scientific standards. Thus, in the first place, psychological experience appears not only as mechanistic but also as purposive. However, such a characteristic is not strictly speaking insurmountable inasmuch as biology and medicine are both purposive and cannot be denied on that basis a right to scientific validity. But purpose in psychology as we have defined it goes far beyond the appearance of purpose if it is restricted to mental operations or biological goals. We have yet to show whether there is purpose in psychological experience itself and whether such purpose is one with biological or mental goals. The problem of purpose converges also towards the problem of the experiencing subject and the transmundane and transpersonal self necessary to an understanding of psychological experience. This means of course that we are left with the problem of deciding whether the application of psychological methods, in accordance with the general principles and conditions imposed on us by the logos of the soul, will differ from scientific logic:

(a) if by science we understand knowledge of the reversibility of causal sequences;

(b) if by science we understand the larger sense of purposive behaviour that is irreversible as in the case of biology, but it will be science if we understand thereby a creative spirit that is both a quest for knowledge and a fostering of develoment. Thus in psychology we are forced to admit that the normative values are part of the essence of methodological procedure. The split which created the science myth is no longer possible because we have to include rather than exclude whatever goals or causes present themselves to us as part of psychological experience whether they be transmundane or intramundane.

Strictly speaking, psychological method is less an analysis than both an analysis and a synthesis at one and the same time. It is both a consolidation and a dissolution. The conditions to be satisfied by this method are as follows:

1. It must apply to psychological experience and not to the medium in which and through which such experience expresses itself such as body, psychoid, or mental fields.

2. Its significance resides not in abstraction and impersonal law but, on the contrary, in concretion and transpersonal or universal personality meanings, of which the individual personality is an instance, just as individual particular phenomena are instances of the universal but impersonal physical law.

3. Its verification therefore takes place by reference to psychological experiences and its truth values by reference to the development of personality.

In psychology therefore the realisation of personality corresponds to what the ideals of control over nature and a world of material comfort correspond to in physical science. The realisation of the transpersonal meaning of personality is analogous to the discovery of law and the possession of knowledge of this world which is the aim of scientific intellect. But whereas in the latter the goal and the method do not essentially condition one another, in the former they do. Therefore in psychology it is of the utmost importance to spend thought on our initial propositions. It is only too clear from the lesson of science that there is a wide discrepancy between its actual achievements and its normative values and idealism which is ever receding before it the more it advances, whereas one of the main driving forces has been that, thanks to its advance, such goals will be closer to us. A misunderstanding or underestimation of this problem will mean that in psychology the more we get to learn about the individual and psycho-physical behaviour along the usual lines of scientific methodology the further away we will move from the soul and the ultimate goals that motivate us to find out about ourselves and others. The more we know the further away we will move from the mystery and realisation of personality.

*

The spirit of science is something that seeks to discover . . . But discovery is not opposed to realisation, which is the best form of discovery. Realisation typifies the soul because it is of the essence of subjectivity and hence corresponds in psychology to what understanding is for the mind and explanation is for physical events.

Science was the expression of our emergence from the dream world of the mythological unconscious. This same spirit of science, transformed, marks our emergence into the light of psychological realities. It also marks the discovery of the soul emerging from the world of affect and of dream into a being and a reality. A new being and reality will completely transform our world picture as science transformed the old symbolical mythical one.

*

It is important to formulate the idea of a specific psychological vocation, corresponding to the value of psychological experience *per se*. This does not invalidate other basic experiences such as the religious and artistic. For those following the latter do not orient themselves towards the psyche *per se* but to the content or objective aspect of a vision. They do not say this vision is a psychic content, just as we do not say this table is a piece of matter. They take it for granted and connect directly to the experience. The reaction itself will determine whether this experience is understood philosophically, religiously, *etc.*

In practising psychotherapy I have no illusions as to what I am doing: I am *practising* a philosophical and extra-mundane activity as much as a purely scientific profane one.

This fact frightens people. It frightens me.

*

Generally the idea is that "Analysis" consists in the analysis of unconscious contents with the purpose of bringing them into consciousness. This making the unconscious conscious has an "integrative" effect on the psyche and dimisinishes the extent of dissociation which may exist thus giving a greater unity of action, and a greater power of absorption, to the personality in general.

However this process is not as simple as it may have looked at the beginning of the new methods. The unconscious is a hypothetical concept of considerable complexity: not only is it divided into independent systems, as with Freud, but we are under the obligation to clarify, modify and extend continually our idea of the unconscious, to meet facts that cannot be explained by the current theories. We are in particular brought up again and again against the cruel fact that we tend to project preformed ideas into the vague and limitless possibilities of such an elusive concept as that of the unconscious.

Therefore the less we systematize and rationalize our theories the better chance we have for an objective observation of psychological phenomena. For it is only when the psyche has been left on its own that we can really see what it has to tell us. On the other hand, such is the chaos and prolixity of psychic phenomena that we can hardly expect to bring scientific clarity into the field unless we do proceed in a systematic and scientifically valid exploration.

In this kaleidoscopic series of events certain definite lines emerge and a certain amount of practical knowledge of the field has been consolidated. This knowledge forms the backbone of our theories and our experience. But as in other disciplines so too in psychology the professional psychologist will not be able to tell you just how he works. His experience is also a matter of instinct, that sort of "instinct" that makes for vocation. However, instinct by itself is not enough and it has to be based on a serious and exhaustive knowledge of the field in question. But once the contemporary theories are assimilated instinct remains an unknown quantity, and the inexhaustible source of new theories, new points of view and daring speculations.

As a result of the confirmation of what instinct lays down, what intuition permits to conceive is attained only through proof provided by experience and by observation of cases. Here too we are in difficult terrain for one case is not enough to establish an interpretation or to permit the formulation of a law. Thus the strange and uncomfortable phenomenon emerges in psychology of a situation where we have as many theories of psychology as there are types and groups of people. The choice of a theory will be the result very often of the psychologist's own personal inclinations. Psychology tends therefore to be divided into schools very much as religious or spiritualist movements divide into sects according to the specific nature of and inclinations of human nature. This situation, though it cannot be considered as invalid, is nevertheless not satisfactory to our scientific ideals that tend towards the discovery of high type generalizations permitting us to subsume all divergencies under the unity of primary simple principles.

It is to the degree that a scientific psychology tends towards this high type generalization that it has the greatest hope for success.

Energy problems or libido problems have been considered under two aspects: the mechanistic by Freud; the energic by Jung.

The mechanistic considers events as occurring between substances or things which modify one another according to strict laws. In a network of such phenomena we choose one series which we consider fundamental to the others. The relations of the latter to this series being discovered we find laws that determine our fields of investigation and bring order into the otherwise random events we have observed.

The energic point of view considers not the events as such but the quantities of energy contained in the event. If we can measure the energy contained in any event and provided a given quantity of energy remains constant, then we can follow the transformation of that quantity of energy through various events. We do not choose one series of events as more fundamental than others; all series are fundamentally the same since the energy quanta are equal. The causal principle is not specific but unspecific and non-hypostasized. The value of this point of view is enormous in so far as it enables us to bring events into our observational field by discovering the laws of the transformation of energy quanta. Hence the titles of Jung's important works, *Symbols of Transformation* and *Transformation of the Libido*. Events of different "kinds" can thus be considered.

There is, however, a third approach to events and particularly psychological events, the qualitative. Connected with the principles of *alloiosis* that fascinated Plato and Aristotle this point of view states that energic transformations are to be seen not as displacements of energy quantities (energic point of view) nor again as the displacement of events (mechanistic), but as changes in the qualities of the field observed. Laws that govern qualitative transformations must exist. And these laws are not to be discovered by reducing quality to quantity, whether this quantity be a non-specific psychic energy or a specific psychic energy.

Qualitative transformation is as fundamental as quantitative and as fruitful. We do not know how a field of phenomena can look from the qualitative point of view and how we can formulate laws at all; scientific logic has simply ignored the possibilities of research in this direction. The materialistic-empirical point of view should not exclude in principle this possibility.

No one denies that psychic manifestations or psychological behaviour is as much a question of quantity as of quality. The ethical value of actions is as important in our judgement of a person's activity as is the intensity and extensity of that activity. Psychological behaviour is the ground of ethical judgements, of philosophical and religious values, as it is for the work of the neurologist, the biologist, the politician, the economist, and the physicist.

If therefore there is a qualitative essence of psychological behaviour there must be a qualitative energy behind these actions. As the latter two views lead us to formulate quantitative views of psychic energy, this third view leads us to a qualitative formulation of psychic behaviour.

Whether we regard energic problems from the mechanistic or the energic points of view, both of these look at the psychic field as a quantity in terms of a manifest act, image or thought, or the possibilities of such (the unconscious).

The mechanistic will tell its tale by weaving the one golden thread of its causal principle through the various threads of observations it has gathered; the energic will tell its tale in terms of all these threads giving to each the value of its intensity and quantity.

Both however are descriptive, the one an atomistic reduction of the complex to the simple or *vice versa,* the other phenomenological, working in terms of complexities and complex descriptions which reveal laws of interconnection and interorganisation that cannot be reduced to simpler atomic facts without losing the essence of the law. The law can only be observed in its complexities, much as we can only observe a rainbow given the atmospheric condition of rainclouds, light, *etc....*

That such laws exist has been abundantly proved by Jung. But the difficulty in following Jung and observing these laws lies in their complex presentation and in the sudden intuitive perception of them (which does not make them less real or objective), like working out the combination of a safe. We do not appreciate how complex this presentation is because we are instinctively and habitually accustomed to read atomic causal factors into our material. Therefore we find the complex material presented to us logically confused or incomprehensible. If we seek to comprehend it we do so by projecting into it all the logic and empiricism of the mechanistic point of view. In addition mere observation of the material is not enough to see the law at work; personal experience is necessary to complete the picture and add conviction to what has been revealed.

Even here we are still dealing with an empiricism determined by quantitative observations and eliminating qualitative judgements as much as possible from the field of observation as well as from its manner of exposition and formulation. We ignore the qualitative aspects of psychic energy. The hypothesis of a qualitative psychic energy, leading to a revision of the principles of scientific procedure, is essential to complete the picture of a quantitative psychic energy. A revision is necessary for many reasons.

Can we in any way formulate, observe, and scientifically control qualitative processes of the psyche?

By "scientifically control" we must understand "make logically plausible and empirically valid", "make logically valid and empirically possible."

A qualitative process of transformation does not mean the transformation of a given quantity of libido from one *form* into another; it means the transformation of one *quality* of libido into another quality of libido. The transformation of such qualities can take place through quantitative events and transformations, but these are incidental to the ultimate goal of process. Incidental though they are, they must be included as important aspects of our picture without which we would be at sea, but we must be constantly on our guard against the strong temptation to follow the easier way of quantitative control and description as though this were the *real* event, whereas this event is only real to the degree that it participates in the transformations of quality that are taking place contemporaneously.

After all, what is our ideal of happiness and our ideal of perfection in this world? Is it that millions and millions should multiply and live in a continuously multiplying nature or is it that those who live should find peace, beauty, and truth? Are our efforts to be concentrated on multiplying matter or in refining and perfecting it? The multiplication of matter leads to chaos and of course in the end it is not the number of people that count because we know that spirit is One and that the soul is also ultimately One, and that in this sense all the millions of souls can live as One soul. This fact is more plausible than the idea that the more millions of souls there are the more we refine and make matter beautiful and perfect. On the contrary, we see now that the multiplication of matter and the indefinite multiplication of biological species leads to disintegration, chaos, and suffocation, forcing man eventually to destroy himself on this earth by overgrowth or to seek beauty and truth in the lifeless and tremendous spaces of the cold stellar galaxies. What a gamble!

Is it really for beauty and truth that man sets sail for the lifeless wastes of the Moon and Mars or is it for the conquest of raw materials and the strategic value of the operation? Is the scientist a slave to the worst in us or is he a server of truth?

*

The value of the archetype cannot be sufficiently appreciated unless it is subsumed under a high level teleological hypothesis. Thus, it is perfectly consonant with this approach to the problem to apply Adlerian teleology to psychological behaviour provided however it forms a lower level concept in the system. There are many archetypal patterns whose goal is certainly not power over the environment.

It is the value of this high-type hypothesis that has escaped the attention of philosophers and logicians critical of psychological concepts. The investigations and material brought together as a result of our psychological researches indicate that there is a common theme to the story book of the archetypes. Converging from many directions and joining together many levels of behaviour and motivation the theme of consciousness weaves its way throughout psychological literature. In this sense, consciousness can be considered as a high-type generalisation of a teleological character. For, we do not know what connection, if any, exists between physico-chemical processes and consciousness, and secondly, we do not know what connection can exist between teleological goals such as domination of the environment, survival, *etc.* and consciousness;

but we do know that time and again our observations lead us to the hypothesis that consciousness is a goal much sought for and arrived at by the most devious and diverse means and under the most various conditions. Since therefore we cannot deduce or infer consciousness as a consequence of causal chains and since the theme of consciousness does turn up from our observations and gives meaning to our material we must infer that consciousness is an hypothesis wide enough to correlate and organise all the other goals and causal connections we have observed into a meaningful whole. The goals of archetypes, the deterministic character of psychological behaviour and causal laws acquire a meaning when organised by the higher type hypothesis of consciousness. But this consciousness is not possible of definition, it is just a goal.

To conclude, although archetypes allow us neither to infer causal laws nor one definite goal-directed activity in terms of a specific goal as in biology where maintenance (self-preservation) or reproduction (species-survival) can be postulated, nevertheless they do have an important descriptive value so that we are better able to organise and better able to predict the course of events. On what law however does such prediction rest if the only laws of prediction are either causal or teleological?

Far from believing, as Jung does, that archetypes need explanation I would say that an archetype is itself the best explanation we can give of the experiences we are dealing with. In so far as the archetype claims our attention it demands as much explanation in the sense of a clarification as a *cultus*, a religious feeling of respect and awe. But for an archetypal explanation to be valid we should be able to predict the future. I believe that such predictions are in fact possible, and that this need not take the form of a prophecy, although it should be noted that predictions on the basis of archetypal knowledge are indeed prophecies and fill most of the contents of apocalyptic and eschatological literature. The sort of prediction I mean is far more modest. On the basis of a constellation of an archetype we can predict the appearance not only of certain correlated themes but also of certain correlated experiences.

In talking of archetypes and prediction I would like to mention that the archetype is conditioned by the psyche as a whole and therefore is ultimately the conditioning factor of psychological experiences. It is not that the archetype is here and the prediction out there. Thus the archetype can be said not only to predict but to prepare the way for the event predicted. In fact it becomes legitimate to doubt whether the event could indeed occur if the archetype is not already constellated; thus what the connection between the archetype and the event predicts is simply the fact the event itself is part of the archetypal content.

The appearance of the child motif for instance enables us to infer a certain psychological state, but this inference is neither built on a knowledge of causal chains between images and coincidences with children (synchronistic phenomena) nor is it built on a teleological explanation. It belongs simply to the observation of a correlation of such themes with certain psychological states. The appearance of the two together need not be explained by any hidden link, mystic power, or teleological purpose, but simply by the fact both are aspects of the archetypal configuration. The problem would then be to what extent the concept of the archetype is explanatory and valid, that is to say, reflects a real structure or an aspect of reality. To that I can say that we do not know except through inferences. But in this sense we do not know either causal laws or teleological explanations. All we do have is a statistical probability quota. And given time the use of the concept of the archetype will, like that of causality, show its validity as a concept interpreting the structure of reality.

Archetypes are to be understood not only in terms of their teleological functions but indeed in terms of conditioning factors as well. In fact we must ask what causes an archetype to appear in such and such a manner and why it appears to compensate or to preclude or to indicate such and such. If we examine the possibility of the conditioning of archetypes we will see that man has a much greater share and responsibility in his destiny than we are willing to admit on the face of the evidence at our disposal. For, if the archetypes with their powerful affective grip can influence and change the course of human destiny and the development of a human being, the possibility that the archetype itself can be changed, conditioned and cultivated becomes important and should be taken seriously. Indeed, is not science itself but the study of the conditions external to man and how man can change the world he lives in by acting upon some of these conditions? He does not change the laws of the cosmos. He interferes in such a way that these laws in continuing to act as they do will produce situations in accordance with the changes he has introduced.

Thus, if archetypes are the psychic structures and laws of psychic life, much as instincts can be said to be those of biological life, then the conditioning of the archetype becomes an important aspect of psychological concern. Are archetypes changed only by trying to understand them, to make them conscious? There is no doubt that these two forces have an exceedingly important causal effect on archetypes. But from the literature, we gather that such collective and powerful emotional forces as are attached to archetypal themes require a certain amount of emotional response. The attempt to understand the archetype should therefore be accompanied by a certain emotional response to the archetype. This emotional response to such themes is almost absent in Protestantism, and it is for this reason that a great deal of the art of dealing with mana-charged themes is almost impossible for the rational and one-sided attitude to life denoted by the modern scientific mind. In fact the modern world has been voided of its symbolic-mythical reality simply because the emotions attached to these have been drained off and have attached themselves to the spirit of scientific curiosity. It seems almost then that to pay an affective courtship to the archetype implies to have little emotional drive left to maintain scientific work. This is almost a Faustian dilemma. Man cannot give the gods their food without which they will die if he has himself eaten of the fruit of knowledge and liked it, that is, has become emotionally attached to it.

Emotion today must be recruited in terms of our quest and commitment to the truth, and the truth not of our own intellect but of the soul and the faith it inspires in us. The faith that our psychology can lead us to the passionate experience of reality and the truth is the only answer to this need to respond emotionally to the experiences of the archetypes and thus change them in our favour.

*

If amplification deserves the name of method of exploration it is because meanings and implications of the image are revealed or discovered. These meanings, moreover, do not necessarily have to be unconscious, but they are psychically significant and interrelated. Bringing them into significant relationships is revelatory and exploratory as well as integrative. The difference between amplification and mere theoretical speculations of meaning is that in amplification the associations are "governed by the emotionally and psychically qualified moment" (Ed. note: Quotation untraceable) and not by reason working alone. In this way each image and each psychic process acquires a "quality", a "life" and character of its own, which is rich and inexhaustible in its significance and emotional values. And these images and psychic processes being repeated both historically and geographically acquire a general life of their own, significant and important, not only to the particular person who at one time in a certain place may have produced them, but to all of us.

Amplification leads to active imagination, to a dialectical relationship with the psyche: Dialectical relationship means that we simply talk to ourselves or, in other words, ask ourselves about certain things. This "self" is not always the conscious ego. Many times people feel that the answer to a problem is within themselves but not quite conscious. They therefore think about it and carry it around with them. During this process they quite often catch themselves talking to themselves. Dialectical relationship, like active imagination, is merely the refinement and objectivation of this natural tendency in each of us. It is raised from the raw material of an everyday occurrence and a spontaneous instinctive process to an art and a technique. When, however, we consider spirit as the central axis or our point of reference these dialectical relationships converge towards one dialectical possibility that governs all others, namely, relationship to God. God is not merely a psychic content of great value, He is also an objective non-psychical reality which may or not talk to us through the psychic image. The dialectical relationship with God, known also as the discrimination of spirits, is a fundamental phenomenon that we cannot equate with the more psychological process of dialectical relationship to the psyche and the unconscious autonomous content opposing or differentiated and cut off from consciousness.

This distinction is important since the problem of dialectical relationships is a great headache and source of confusion to psychologists as well as to theologians. To talk with oneself borders on lunacy. And, moreover, what is the criterion? However scientific and cautious we may be in such a process, the problem remains that when I talk to some "other" within me and I believe and respond to it, I also want to believe that it is what it is, *i.e.*, real, and in particular whether it is a spirit and not just a psychic content. But the clarity of spirit, its objective value, is often confused in the beginning and certainly not evident. This is what tradition means by "clarification" or "purification" of the spirit that appears as "material" and is weighed down by the heavy, dark matter of ignorance and psychic contents still contaminated by the body.

We must therefore suppose that psychic contents are not absolutes but themselves "obscure". Thus we are preserved from ascribing to them any absolute value but only a relative one, relative to the state not only of our consciousness but of the subtlety and purity of the psyche itself. This purification of the psyche, rather than the purification of the spirit, is indicated by the purification and washing of Lato. The psyche is Woman whereas the spirit is Man. And though both need purifying, the process is quite independent at the beginning. The psychological significance of events is a different thing from their spiritual meaning.

There is no doubt moreover that the purification of the psyche is a process from below upwards while that of spirit is one from up down. This means that the energy at our disposal for the purification and objectification of psychic contents is no other than the biological energy locked in the body and in instinctive patterns. Whereas the activation of the spirit is experience as an "intrusion", something coming to us from "without", in short a "grace" which we "receive", that of the body is experienced as an awakening from within, a liberation of energy that is of the body and the instincts and in particular of sexuality.

Therefore it should not be surprising that, when a spiritual meaning touches us, the first response to this is a sexual one, an awakening of dormant instinctive potentialities. That is why spirit and sex are so closely connected and prove such a disconcerting problem to man. Now if the problem of this creation was the redemption of the soul only, then there would be no reason for bodily existence at all. If, on the other hand, the soul's sin and ignorance is due to its existence in the body, then the redemption of the soul must involve dealing with the body since it is the body that is the "dark" part, the source or evidence of its ignorance. Thus, in either case the body is not omitted, and whether we talk of the redemption of the body (the second resurrection) or whether we talk of the redemption of the soul, in both cases the physical universe is included. Psychologically this means there is no redemption of the soul without a redemption of instinct. But the redemption of instinct is contained within instinct. This means that instinct is a carrier of a purpose. Hence, too, our disinclination to condemn instinct, and our inclination to throw the blame rather on the misuse and abuse of instinct. The full dynamism of "instinct" can never be realised unless instinct is liberated from its compulsive patterns. The agent producing this liberation is instinct itself. It is to this purpose that *meditation* should be oriented and its techniques adapted. And since the ego has no say in the matter, the attitude to adopt is to be detached but interested, active in non-action. Purity of purpose and submission to spirit are necessary for the security and control of the enormously powerful potential of instinctive force released, blind as it is, and dangerously chaotic.

*

... What you say about spirit calls for an answer. I believe that the ideas you express are important, but they tempt one to go into two mutually exclusive directions, the way of philosophy and the way of psychology. The important thing, it seems to me, is to make clear that what one believes will have an effect upon one's psychological experience and this in turn on psychological development as a whole. Now, although the clarification of such beliefs requires a great deal of clear thinking, it is not for the sake of that thinking but for the ulterior effect that the ideas arrived at will have on the soul. Put it slightly differently and say that part of the process of psychic development consists in making ideas that are hazy, unclear or outright unconscious, clear and concise. But without the help of reason, the *lumen naturae,* we have no guide to give form to this psychic development, because once these ideas are conscious they require qualitative evaluation and this is a matter of the intellect which itself springs from basic attitudes to the world, to life, and to the soul. Jung's psychology, or rather the exponents of psychic development *per se,* underestimate this fact. Of course, there is a certain justification for this attitude in so far as they place themselves in a cultural situation which has consistently undervalued the psyche and overvalued the mind for the sake of the mind. Hence the cry, first experience the psyche and then talk. But also the counter cry, once I have experienced the psyche what will guarantee the necessary discrimination? And here the silent trust in a "psychological natural growth" crops up. It is believed that the psyche, once it is really accepted, will create its own intellectual discrimination. This silent and tacit belief is another instance of what you have called the biological lens: as mind evolves out of the primal cell, so spirit evolves out of the psyche. Hence trust the psyche and the rest will follow. I believe this to be but a half-truth, namely, that we must experience and trust the psyche but that this does not imply that the rest which will follow is necessarily of the spirit. Now no one in antiquity or in the East has ever said "trust the soul" no matter how much he believed in the soul. For the *idea,* trust the soul, is an example of one of these fundamental premises that live in the half light. Most people who have had some experience in this matter and have left us testimonies have always said "trust the spirit" and they have said it over and above those who maintained a blind trust in nature or a superstitious awe of the psyche and so called occult phenomena. However, people today, when they say "trust the spirit", immediately use this as an excuse to undervalue both the soul and the body. We must therefore dig deep into the forces at work. To illustrate this statement I would take up the theme you discuss.

The idea of the birth of spirit from matter is either the consequence of, or the result of the idea that biological instinct can be transformed into a higher counterpart. Freud talks of transformation as a sublimation, meaning that there is a mere substitution of the final goals, a canalisation, while the primary discharge takes place in both cases. Jung, very rightly in his early days, pointed out that we cannot interpret this transformation as a mere substitution of goals but that there was a qualitative change which has to be accounted for. Hence, the idea of culture as a qualitative transformation of basic biological drives. What distinguishes culture from mere substitution is the presence of the leaven of spirit. However, a closer examination of Jung's premises shows us that the matter of spirit has been brought in as a *consequence* of his argument, and not as a fundamental attitude to experience. The fundamental attitude remains humanistic, his fundamental experience is human culture, not spirit. Spirit is accepted but only as a function of this attitude. And now I would dare say that this attitude means just as much as Freud's does, *that the body is ultimately denied.* Hence modern science is a "concretion" of this denial since its main results are to *destroy material.* It is therefore the rightful heir of the primary *act of denial* initiated by modern times.

I do not know whether it is the denial of the body that creates the justificatory philosophy or the other way around. In so far as Protestantism is prior to psychology and science as we know them, it would seem to me, at first glance, that the denial of the body is the primary move from which the rest follows. How is the body denied, you will ask? Well, it's quite simple since, if you hold the view that biological instinct is in need of transformation, or again if you regard nature as transforming herself from lower biological forms to higher cultural ones, you have already condemned instinct and nature. There is already a judgment. Now, if you say, but of course an integration of the biological fact is necessary not a repression or a denial as do both Jung and Freud, you have not changed the fundamental premiss of your approach. Call it what you will, "integration", "sublimation", "transformation", "assimilation", there is always the idea of a judgement and an evaluation, at the expense of the totality of the natural fact. In other words, the natural biological man is always one element of the picture, the other is the mental, social, cultured, spiritual man. We then create ideas of uniting the two or transforming the one into the other (Freud). But this is a gross error. The biological man including his mind and his consciousness, however developed and "evolved" these be, is the *whole picture.* Spirit can only come from "outside" and "into" this picture; it can never be talked about as another term of the picture.

Putting it in theological terms, Christ's humanity is not accepted as it is, but has to be changed into something more perfect, more consonant with the *idea* of divinity. Or, again, the world is not what it is, but has to be changed into something else. Hence there arises what we may call the passion to change things, and we psychologists suffer from a peculiarly acute form of this passion, namely, the desire to change people and ourselves. At bottom, such a passion is the human will playing at god; a spiritual passion monopolised by an unregenerate intellect. Hence, when we make these ideas clear, we purify the intellect. Philosophy is such a purification. If we allow ourselves to be caught by them and directed by them in the unconscious, we succumb to the folly and the illusion that has modern man in its nets, namely, that we are progressing, that nature is becoming something better and higher all the time. Enough of all this.

These ideas are the more convincing since I have had to arrive at them through experience. To survive I have had to sacrifice the psychological interpretations of things and people and face them as they are; I have learned that the passion to control a situation by changing it or the people is an evil not a good. People are what they are and have to be met with on that level. Then I see suddenly that I, too, am what I am and meet myself on that level as will. The hero myth dissolves.

I have been reading some Karl Jaspers recently and finding him rather good. Also interested very much in Dilthey, Spranger and German "Geisteswissenschaft Psychologie". They seem to think on my lines with this difference, that they have left the "psyche" out of the picture. It is funny how *men* are always seeking to bypass the soul in their attempt to get a shortcut to spirit.

*

The psyche is not inside man, it is we who are inside the psyche...

*

Must pay great attention to the European Christian prejudice which at bottom has contempt for the East while professing to understand and sympathise with it on the surface...

The difference between eastern doctrines and Christianity is that the latter takes its point of departure from the ego. Man identifies himself with the conscious ego and takes upon himself the sin of separateness, ignorance and illusion that is the ego. Thus the Spirit is the Other, is outside him, and the soul too exists only as a function of the ego. This position is not wrong provided man accepts this identification and its consequences. Consider another solution: His repentance and contrition would be just as valid if he were to objectify the ego and not identify with it thus making it the cause of ignorance. Then the ego is not killed but exists as an independent entity that has to be uprooted. In both cases what is important is to accept the responsibility and to perform the task required to this purpose.

The Easterner chooses the second and the ego becomes an unconscious and autonomous complex which can well be the source of disturbing influences and which certainly has to be faced if his claim to spiritual realisation is to have any validity. To the Westerner, on the other hand, it is the spirit and soul that become unconscious disturbing factors with a claim on his attention. If he disregards this claim, he is soon made aware of it by symptoms and accidents.

In both cases the work of purification is necessary, but whereas the Easterner suffers the ego passively and ascribes its evil to karma and past deeds, the Westerner is actively identified with it and therefore necessarily takes on its evil and is overwhelmed by the sense of its guilt. This passivity to the ego makes the Easterner tend to repress the ego as an evil and the individuation process as wholly undesirable, and so puts him off the track. The Westerner, on the other hand, gets suddenly fed up with all this talk of sin and tends to emphasize the fact that after all man is not evil. Both these reactions risk missing the point; it is not a question of accepting the ego passively or actively, but one of detaching oneself from it by following the natural process of spiritual development vivified by Grace.

※

I believe that we must make a distinction between functions of consciousness when the contents refer to mundane considerations and when they refer to extramundane beliefs. Unfortunately this distinction, though generally agreed, is not entirely kept in Jung's writings where the type problem tends to become a sort of absolute structure of the psyche and hence metaphysical.

This is understandable because any theory of types and functions of apprehension and evalution of reality necessarily weakens the truth values of philosophical and ethical systems. For a philosophical system that is analysed in terms of its "type" cannot be absolute in any way and the relativising of its contents would be strongly objected to by its adherents. Problems of types only too readily degenerate into *ad hominem* arguments. Conversely, if the type analysis is convincing, then the values of the philosophical ideas are transferred and attach themselves to the types so that the latter acquire, so to speak, the aura of the former.

There are many theories of types and Jung's is in no way more absolute than the others. On the other hand, the analysis of philosophical, theological and metaphysical material in terms of Jung's types necessarily goes beyond the relative limits of scientific hypotheses to make claims of actual psychic ultimate structures. I confess that I am attracted by the pull of this psychologism, and recognise, however, that the only way to save face is to admit that in this respect at least we are indeed doing more than science and that there is apparently nothing wrong with this provided we do not seek to mislead or to dupe ourselves.

Thus, it seems to me that the problem of types requires, if it is to be effective, the sacrifice of the values of philosophy. Personally I am not ready for that yet, although it is becoming clear to me that I will eventually have to effect this sacrifice if I am to be wholly committed to psychology.

Now it seems to me, moreover, that the problems of our destiny, the problems of extramundane life, are so sweeping and pressing and claim so much of the whole man that the problem of types seems hardly able to fit in at all. For types present an ideal situation that is not so ideal unless it is actually realised. But it is the problems of this realisation, what religiously minded people would call redemption, that concern us most. Now, are processes of redemption or salvation in any way concerned with intramundane problems of functions and types? For instance, if all my functions were activated, would there still be a problem of redemption? I believe there would. On the other hand, somehow there must be connection between the two. But this would be so only on the basis of the ultimate reality of the soul and then function would actually refer to a state of redemption of the body and of this world, hence extramundane.

*

The way of individuation is unique, but the goal is not. The mistake that people make is to make the goal one's "own unique" individualised self, where this is the instrument and not the goal.

*

What gives soul to people is the capacity to experience the paradox of life.

*

The consciousness of his mortality leads a man to revolt or else seek a way out. The consciousness of mortality is itself a luciferian act or perhaps the result of one. Yet it is not mortality conscious of itself but the immortal man conscious of himself and his mortal shadow which he has to accept. (This is, of course, my mistake for it is precisely the consciousness of its own mortality that gives any effectiveness and meaning to the ego's acceptance of its own death. This interpretation of mine shows that I had still to pass through the fire ... it was written a long time ago and before the ordeal.) "What is projected into the snake must therefore be the consciousness of his own mortality, or else why seek a way out?" (The Koran)

ZURICH-ALEXANDRIA

104

Selected Titles from the **Dunquin Series:**
Rare monographs and translations, symbolism, and depth psychology

The Homeric Hymns
Charles Boer, tr.

Since 1972, this version of the *Homeric Hymns*—nominated for the National Book Award—has been acclaimed by critics and public and has widely established itself as a classroom text. These thirty-five poems are the earliest extant depiction of the Gods and Goddesses as individual figures. Boer's translation is a fresh and stunning experience, offering immediate access to the archetypal characters of the Greek pantheon.   vi, 182 pp.   ISBN 210–0

Goddesses of Sun and Moon
Karl Kerenyi

A colleague of C. G. Jung's and one of the major mythographers of this century here takes a novel look at four unusual feminine configurations depicted in Greek mythology. The vision that emerges restores passionate feminine consciousness to its rightful place both in politics and in the economy of the psyche. The four papers—exploring the mythemes of Circe, the enchantress; Medea, the murderess; Aphrodite, the golden one; and Niobe of the Moon—together lend a deep psychological orientation to some of the most puzzling, controversial issues of our day: feminism, the occult, aesthetics, madness, dreams, even terrorism.   84 pp.   ISBN 211–9

Avicenna and the Visionary Recital
Henry Corbin

For imaginal psychologists—and it was Corbin who coined the term "imaginal"—and for all concerned with symbolic thinking and religious consciousness as the foundation of consciousness itself. Presenting here a symbolic journey of Avicenna, the great Persian physician and mystic, Corbin unfolds its fantastic imagery in such a way as to relate it to the timeless concerns of every soul, whether ancient or modern. His piety, humor, fearless intuition, and scrupulous scholarship create a new kind of text that is both difficult and clear, classical and profoundly relevant. Bibliography, index.   314 pp.   ISBN 213–5

An Anthology of Greek Tragedy
Albert Cook, Edwin Dolin, eds.

The major Greek plays, including *The Trojan Women, The Bacchae,* both *Oedipus* tragedies, etc. Aeschylus, Sophocles, Euripides *together* in one volume. Each of the eight translations in large, clear print by a contemporary published scholar-poet. The broadly informative and readable introduction (35 pp.) covers the field, while each play is also prefaced, adding depth and detail. With numbered lines for locating quotations, maps, theater plans, bibliographies. This excellent reference, beautiful and accurate, provides a single-volume way to enter the Greek world at the roots of Western culture.   xl, 403 pp.   ISBN 215–1

Apollo—Four Studies
Karl Kerenyi

Apollo—a popular favorite among Greek deities and yet most misunderstood of divine concepts. Here is the original Apollo, a mysterious light-and-dark force revealed by the renowned psychological mythographer Karl Kerenyi. Four chapters examine Apollonian cult, myth, and thought, ranging through such disparate symbols as the serpents at Delphi, the broom of Ion, the swans of the *Phaedo,* and the winds of the North.   76 pp.   ISBN 216–X

ISBN prefix 0–88214
Spring Publications, Inc. • Box 222069 • Dallas, TX 75222